TO BE
GIFTED
&
LEARNING
DISABLED

From Identification to Practical Intervention Strategies

Susan M. Baum, Ph.D.

Steve V. Owen, Ph.D.

John Dixon, Ph.D.

Creative Learning Press, Inc.

P.O. Box 320, Mansfield Center, Connecticut 06250

PRINTED IN THE UNITED STATES OF AMERICA
ISBN 0-936386-59-2

CONTENTS

PREFACE

> There's a land that I see
> Where the children are free.
> And I say it's not far
> To this land from where we are.
> Come with me
> Take my hand and we'll live—
> In a land where the river runs free
> In a land through the green country
> In a land to a shining sea
> Where you and I are free to be
> You and me.
>
> (Lawrence, S. & Hart, B., 1972)

Wouldn't it be wonderful if this land were as near as the neighborhood school where all our nation's young could indeed grow and become. Unfortunately, for some of our children, school is far from liberating. In fact, it may be rather restrictive where the learning environment is based on the teacher's needs rather that the needs of individual students. In this most restrictive environment, the curriculum is often determined before knowledge of the individual students, their interests, and their learning style preferences are discovered. Lessons are apt to be taught to all children in the same way with student evaluations primarily contingent upon written products. In this kind of school, exciting curriculum is often reserved for those preciously few moments when basic skills are finally mastered. In short, because school is a place where reading, writing and arithmetic are highly valued over other gifts and talents, nonreaders or poor writers are rarely given the time or opportunity to run free to that shining sea.

There are some students who suffer considerably form this most restrictive world because they cannot conform to particular kinds of learning. By definition they are a strange paradox—they have special intellectual gifts but are unsuccessful with certain basic learning tasks. This group, in particular, is at great risk for developing its potential because the major focus of educational intervention is on what the students do not know and cannot do rather than on nurturing their talents.

These students are often classified as learning disabled, and, by law, their education must take place in the least restrictive environment. Ironically, the resulting plan often becomes so restrictive that these youngsters have little chance of reaching their potential because they are not allowed the freedom to learn in a way that accentuates who they are. Because we are concerned about the future of these bright youngsters, we have written this book.

The research, ideas and practical suggestions contained within these pages represent years of our combined study of and interactions with this special population of students. We have witnessed exciting changes in motivation, confidence, and achievement when the learning environment is designed to meet the needs of individual students and to nurture their individual talents. As you explore the words within, we invite you to consider the possibilities of making school a place where

> Every boy in this land
> Grows to be his own man
> In this land every girl
> Grows to be her own woman...
> Where you and I are free to be
> You and me!

PART ONE

Who Are the Gifted Learning Disabled?

CHAPTER 1

INTRODUCTION

How can a child learn and not learn at the same time? Why do some students apply little or no effort to school tasks while they commit time and considerable effort to demanding, creative activities outside of school? These behaviors describe GIFTED, LEARNING-DISABLED (GLD) students. Indeed, discovering answers to these questions will unlock the unique mysteries of students who are bright but learning-disabled. The answers will also clarify the dilemma these students face daily in coping with the paradox of school failure and creative achievement.

We'd like to introduce you to three young people who have suffered the consequences of being bright and creative, yet unsuccessful in school. The stories of these students vividly depict the striking inconsistencies in the behavior of GLD students. By examining the commonalities shared by the three, we can begin to understand the frustration and confusion experienced not only by the students themselves, but by all who interact with them. We can begin to appreciate the need for more information about their characteristics and how we might help these special students to succeed.

Neil

"School is like a basketball game, totally irrelevant to life," spouted a high school student who was daily experiencing failure in school. This analogy unfortunately was true for Neil. School, like basketball, became irrelevant to him when it failed to address or to satisfy any of his needs.

His teachers described Neil as lazy, claiming that he could do much better if he applied himself: "When I talk to Neil, he has so much to offer. But he just doesn't produce." His fellow classmates, applauding his cleverness, viewed Neil as the class clown. Neil saw himself as a misfit. The inconsistencies of his own abilities, his interpretation of people's perceptions of him, and his own feeling of inadequacy totally frustrated Neil.

Neil began to experience difficulty in school in the fourth grade. As he proceeded through the grades, he accomplished less and less. By the time he reached high school, he was in such a depressed emotional state that weekly psychological counseling became necessary. The psychologist suggested an educational evaluation. The results of the evaluation concluded that Neil had learning disabilities that were manifested in difficulty in written organization and sequential tasks for math and algebra.

Accordingly, Neil's curriculum was adjusted. He received supplemental instruction. Special provisions were made in testing and assignments. These are procedures usually recommended for learning-disabled students. However, unlike most learning-disabled students who begin to experience success and start to feel better about themselves, Neil became depressed. He felt that his better grades depended on the school's making concessions for him in light of his specific learning disabilities, even though his school successes were merely watered-down versions of what other bright students could accomplish. In fact, he did not view his achievements as successes at all.

To understand why Neil felt frustrated and unfulfilled even though his grades improved, it is necessary to learn more about him. He is a very sensitive, perceptive and creative child with high intelligence. His concerns were of a global nature, transcending the typical concerns of high school students. For instance, Neil did not see the value in spending time playing intramural sports when he could capture peoples' expressive moods with his camera. However, because he did not like sports, he was considered strange and not accepted as one of the group. He anguished in the realization that he was being judged by his weaknesses, assessed by how he compared to others. Neil had always prided himself in nonconformity in his interests, perceptions and values. To achieve, and thus become more like his peers, was unsettling.

In a sense, "being his own person" allowed Neil to remove himself from competition. This existed in school only; at home the pressure increased. He was constantly competing with the achievements of a highly successful father and a gifted younger brother. Furthermore, his cultural background placed a high priority on achievement and college entry.

Although Neil seemed to resist traditional modes of achievement, on his own he had acquired an enormous wealth of knowledge; he pursued his extracurricular interests with enthusiasm and commitment. He ran his own business as an entrepreneur and photographer. His photography won awards in amateur contests and he was asked to photograph weddings and social events. He taught himself to play the piano and guitar and spent hours playing for his own amusement. Little wonder that he was unable to accept the claim of impaired ability to learn when, to the contrary, he learned so much better on his own.

Photography best unleashed Neil's creative and insightful self. The statements that he made with the camera were powerful and showed his depth of feelings as shown in the photographic essay: "How I Feel About School," pictured on page 4.

But schools put high stock in the written word even when it describes isolated, unrelated, and sometimes irrelevant information.

Would not simply using photography as an option for writing ease this conflict? Unfortunately, the solution is not as simple as tailoring curriculum to the interests of GLD students, especially when their own efforts have resulted in failure for so long. When, in fact, the school allowed Neil to substitute photographic essays for papers, he stopped taking pictures altogether, declaring, "Why can't I be like the piano player in Salinger's *Catcher in the Rye* who used the piano for his own pleasure?" Photography was Neil's escape, an activity over which he had complete control. He did not want teachers to evaluate his photography by standards set up by others. In essence, Neil asked for attention to strengths in their own right, not as a means to work through weaknesses.

Jimmy

Nine-year-old Jimmy flopped down next to his dad and declared, "I'm going to sign my contract to conduct research and start a campaign to get kids to wear bicycle helmets. I know it will be hard, and some days I won't feel like working, but it's such an important project." Starting that day Jimmy became a researcher. His study became his primary focus. After a visit to a professor in measurement and evaluation at a local university, Jimmy concluded that he would follow the professor's suggestion and add some open-ended questions to his survey and include adults in his sample. "I just can't wait to collect my data!"

Jimmy, a fourth-grader, had been diagnosed as mentally retarded during his preschool years. His parents were told that his cognitive development was delayed, and his potential was, well, uncertain. When Jimmy started school, new testing showed that he had at least average intellectual ability, but he experienced great difficulty in learning to read. He was especially clever at avoiding writing. A thorough assessment by a team of educational specialists showed that Jimmy had an attention deficit disorder and problems in reading and writing. His full-scale IQ on the *Wechsler Intelligence Scale for Children, Revised (WISC-R)* (Wechsler, 1974) was 134 with a verbal score of 133 and performance IQ score of 129.

Jimmy hated school and often complained of headaches and stomachaches to avoid completing tasks or coming to school. In school his concentration was limited, distracted by everything and everyone. Can this immature, negative youngster be the young, motivated researcher described above? What explains these wild discrepancies? What could bring better balance to Jimmy's academic efforts and interests?

Photographic Essay
How I Feel About School

School is an ugly geometric existence.

I feel that school has
turned its back on me.

For me, school is a
stepping-stone to nowhere.

I know graduation is the light
at the end of the tunnel.

Because it is irrelevant to life, it's but
pieces of unconnected tracks,
connecting nothing with nothing.

If I do make it out, what will
I have gained? I feel like
a barren tree, still reaching...

* Reprinted with permission from The Council for Exceptional Children. Originally in "Recognizing Special Talents in Learning-Disabled Students," by S. Baum and R. Kirschenbaum in *Teaching Exceptional Children*, Winter 1984, pp. 92–97.

Jimmy's research interests were sparked in his special enrichment program where attention focused on strengths and interests, not on deficits and remediation. Jimmy did complete his research and presented his results to the police department. His poster display of the research showing the need for bicycle helmets was displayed in a local bicycle shop. Jimmy's parents and teachers reported positive changes in his attitude, motivation and achievement that year. His fourth-grade teacher noted that "Jim finally feels that he has the ability to achieve and is putting forth greater effort in reading and writing." His parents could not believe the change in Jimmy's attitude about school, especially on Wednesdays, the day of the program. "We don't even need to set the alarm on his enrichment day. He's up early, prepared and eager to get to school."

Debby

Feeling alone, rejected and depressed, nine-year-old Debby had terrible difficulty making and keeping friends. She was knowledgeable and beyond her years in understanding the injustices of society. World hunger, child abuse, and death occupied her thoughts and conversations. Her dramatic flair in communicating her ideals only served to alienate her classmates who were already confused about Debby's inability to read and write. This sensitive, perceptive young "actress" could only reach out to adults. Unfortunately, her over-dependence on them was often met with further rejection.

Predictably, Debby's self-esteem was dangerously low (at the third percentile on a widely used measure). Her teacher described her as defiant, distrustful and easily hurt. She lacked confidence, concentration and independence when approaching school tasks. Her short attention span and sharp deficits in reading and writing, despite a full-scale IQ score of 128 (Verbal IQ=119, Performance IQ=132) on the *WISC-R*, confirmed the presence of a learning disability. Debby had received remedial support in school since the first grade. Although her basic skills improved somewhat, her emotional well-being in school withered each year.

Participation in the special enrichment pro-

gram during fourth grade proved to be a turning point for Debby. "I never thought I'd be able to create my own slide and tape show. Is it really going to be shown at the museum?" Her eyes sparkled as Debby recounted her role as a director, writer and actress in her historical research, "A Day in the Life of Jerusha Webster," a project she attacked steadily for ten weeks. Her excitement in researching, acting and producing this project resulted in a sense of pride, confidence and accomplishment. To complete the slide show, Debby had to coordinate audio and visual information. Because it was impossible to coordinate it all in school, Debby put it together at home, recruiting her six-year-old sister as a lieutenant.

Debby's classmates were astonished with the finished project. A new respect for her abilities permeated the room. Most importantly, Debby finally seemed to believe in herself!

The Problem

Anecdotal (and sometimes mythical) stories have told of people with crazy-quilt patterns of strengths and weaknesses. Only recently have we begun to study carefully people who have this curious mix of learning disabilities and gifts. It is becoming apparent that when the educational focus is on talent, dramatic changes occur in motivation, self-esteem, and behavior. Traditionally however, students who demonstrate a substantial discrepancy between performance and ability are diagnosed as learning-disabled. Once identified, learning-disabled students are provided with remediation in deficit areas with little or no attention given to strengths. In fact, the students diagnosed as learning disabled who also exhibit superior abilities are offered the same remedial menu as their average-ability, learning-disabled peers. Is the menu equally suitable for the two groups? Or do GLD students have unique characteristics which suggest alternate educational practices?

As suggested by these case studies, sole attention to deficits can be self-defeating to a child who has special talents. In fact, these youngsters appear to need both remediation and enrichment and frequently special counseling to help them understand the paradox in which they must learn to succeed.

A Look Ahead

We have just seen the wild patterns of accomplishment and failure of GLD students. In the remainder of Part I, we provide more background information essential for understanding the GLD youngster. In Chapter 2 we consider the brief history of two traditionally separate fields: giftedness and learning disabilities. We show that the disagreements within and between these fields have promoted confusion about who the GLD child is, and if such a child even exists! In Chapter 3 we describe several pioneering studies of GLD students and use those results to forge a clearer approach to educational intervention.

In Part II of this book, we discuss contemporary psychological theory and research that steer educational applications for GLD students. This section helps to understand the odd patterns of accomplishment and failure that characterize these children, and it creates the foundation for educational interventions discussed later in the book. Chapter 4 describes theories of motivation and considers why the GLD student shows great enthusiasm for certain projects and disdain for others. In Chapter 5 we discuss recent approaches to cognition. Here applications of memory are discussed and tied to behavior. Chapter 6 proposes that intellectual patterns help to understand GLD behaviors. We use two case studies to show how WISC-R subscale scores may be used to predict which sorts of learning activities will and will not succeed.

In Part III, we consolidate information from the first two parts into practical strategies for planning and teaching. Chapter 7 discusses the use of formal and informal assessment techniques for discovering talent and weaknesses of GLD students. In Chapter 8 we offer components and criteria for developing a successful GLD program and describe various programs currently in place. In Chapter 9 we discuss specific motivational and cognitive strategies that aim toward both academic and affective behaviors. We conclude by suggesting resources that will be especially useful to the practitioner in working with GLD students.

CHAPTER 2

A MATTER OF DEFINITION

For many, the terms *learning disabilities* and *giftedness* are at opposite ends of a learning spectrum. Uneasiness in accepting this seeming contradiction in terms stems primarily from faulty ideas and incomplete understandings of each term. This is not surprising since the experts in each of these domains have much difficulty in reaching definitional agreement. Before we attempt to describe the student who is both gifted and learning-disabled, we need an understanding of the two individual parts. These understandings will form the foundation on which the ideas in this book are built.

Historical Perspective of
Learning Disabilities

Learning disabilities as a syndrome began to appear in the literature as early as 1947 with the appearance of Strauss and Lehtinen's book, *Psychopathology and Education of the Brain-Injured Child.* According to the authors, learning deficits could be traced to some minimal brain injury incurred before, during or after birth which may result in defects of the neuromotor system. Children diagnosed as brain-injured demonstrated problems in perception, perseveration or behavior.

Many educators and psychologists objected to the use of the term "brain-injured." Thus in 1957, Stevens and Birch referred to these learning disorders as Strauss' Syndrome. In addition they laid out the defining behaviors in a more observable form:

1. Erratic and inappropriate behavior on mild provocation,

2. Increased motor activity disproportionate to the stimulus,
3. Poor organization of behavior,
4. Distractibility of more than ordinary degree under ordinary conditions,
5. Persistent faulty perceptions,
6. Persistent hyperactivity, and
7. Awkwardness and consistently poor motor performance.

The focus on neurological problems, underlying causes, and resulting behavior gained support during the early sixties. Learning-disabled populations were defined as students who had at least average intelligence and were experiencing difficulties learning because of neurological dysfunction or central processing disorders whether or not specific brain damage could be verified (Clements, 1966; Cruickshank, 1966; Chalfant and Schefflin, 1969). Educational programs were designed to structure the environment to minimize distractions and provide perceptual and motor training to aid in learning.

In the mid-sixties, some researchers were becoming more dissatisfied with this medically-oriented perspective. They found terms like *brain injury* and *central processing disorders* useless in meaning and practice. They preferred using terms to directly describe deficiencies in underlying abilities. Kirk (1963) first used the term *learning disabilities* to describe children who demonstrated developmental disorders in language, speech, reading and communication skills, and excluded children whose learning problems could be attributed to sensory, intellectual or emotional disturbance. Kirk and his colleagues argued that most learning disabilities resulted from underlying language learning problems, which in turn were based on some perceptual difficulties.

Remediation depended on determination of strengths and weaknesses in sensory processing systems. If auditory memory was found to be deficient, visual programs to train memory and teach basic skills were chosen. Remediation also included activities specifically designed to strengthen weak underlying abilities. Typically, these were identified in terms of how the learner received information, processed it and retrieved knowledge and produced new information. Terms such as *reception, closure, sound-symbol associations,* and *memory* were popular among these theorists.

During the decade of the seventies, behaviorist ideas were gaining in popularity and practice. Analysis of underlying causes and discussion of processing deficits are replaced by addressing the direct remediation of basic skills. Efforts to determine why students were not learning were redirected to train teachers how to break down learning into small tasks as a means of enabling students to master specific objectives in curricular areas. This new emphasis implied that deficits in academic skills could be eased by simply reteaching pupils and reinforcing new learning. The cause of the deficit and student intrinsic motivation toward learning mattered little and diverted attention from the real problem: unacceptable behaviors.

The behaviorist position caused major dissension among theorists. Those who favor neurological and underlying processes points of view suggest that a learning disability is relatively permanent in nature and may influence life-long learning and adjustment. Correcting a given skill does not erase difficulty in learning. The behaviorist does not conjecture about future learning, but deals with observable behaviors as they present themselves, and argues that present learning will assure future success (Bloom, cited in *Chance,* 1987). For the proponents of the more permanent view, education tends to focus on compensation strategies, strengthening processing skills, and acquisition of basic skills. In fact, the question arises for non-behavioral professionals whether children assisted through a pure basic skills approach were truly learning-disabled to begin with or were perhaps improperly taught.

This widening rift among professionals contin-

ued to divide the field until the mid-seventies when considerable effort was expended to assure appropriate education for all handicapped children. Hope reigned high that a federal definition would silence the on-going debate in the field of learning disabilities. In 1975, after much debate and compromise, the federal government passed PL 94–142 (The Education for All Handicapped Children Act),. This act defined categories of exceptionality and mandated appropriate identification and educational procedures. The learning-disabled were now defined as

> ...those children who have a disorder in one or more of the basic psychological processes involved in understanding or in using language, spoken or written, which disorder may manifest itself in imperfect ability to listen, think, speak, read, write, spell or do mathematical calculations. Such disorders include such conditions as perceptual handicaps, brain injury, minimal brain dysfunction, dyslexia and developmental aphasia. Such a term does not include children who have learning problems which are primarily the result of visual, hearing, or motor handicaps, of mental retardation, of emotional disturbance, or of environmental , curtural, or economic disadvantage.

> A team may determine that a child has a specific learning disability if (1) the child does not achieve commensurate with his or her age and ability levels in one or more areas [seven of which are specified— oral or written expression, listening comprehension, basic reading skill or comprehension, mathematics calculation or reasoning] when provided with learning experiences appropriate for the child's age and ability levels; and (2) the team finds that a child has a severe discrepancy between achievement and intellectual ability in one or more of [these] areas. (*Federal Register,* 1977, p.65).

This official definition neither eliminated disagreement in the field of learning disabilities (Hammill, Leigh, McNutt, & Larson, 1981; Poplin, 1981), nor gave clear direction in identification issues (Kavale & Nye, 1981; Olson & Mealor, 1981; Harbar, 1981). Instead it raised a host of new questions that contributed to further confusion. For example,

1. How great should the discrepancy be before an individual is considered learning-disabled?
2. Why are only children considered in the definition? What about adults?
3. Do all learning disabilities involve central

nervous system dysfunctions or problems with psychological processes?

4. Cannot handicapped or disadvantaged children have learning disabilities?

Furthermore, most schools today do not follow the federal definition. For example, in a study examining the characteristics of eight hundred identified learning-disabled students, it was found that fewer than half of the students exhibited characteristics consistent with the federal and state definition (Shepard, *et al.* 1983). It appears that currently many schools use their own interpretation of federal and state definitions to select children from their individual districts who they feel are in most need of service regardless of whether a specific learning disability can be identified. In actuality then, learning-disabled students identified in schools represent a fairly heterogeneous group of students with different needs and expectations.

To combat this confusion brought about by the federal definition and local practices, professional organizations have offered their own definitions: The following was adopted by the National Joint Committee for Learning Disabilities:

Learning disabilities is a generic term that refers to a heterogeneous group of disorders manifested by significant difficulties in the acquisition and use of listening, speaking, reading, writing, reasoning or mathematical abilities. These disorders are intrinsic to the individual and presumed to be due to central nervous system dysfunction. Even though a learning disability may occur concomitantly with other handicapping conditions (*e.g.*, sensory impairment, mental retardation, social and emotional disturbance) or en-

National Joint Committee for Learning Disabilities' Definition of Learning Disabilities

Learning disabilities is a generic term	"The Committee felt that *learning disabilities* was a global ('generic') term under which a variety of specific disorders could be reasonably grouped."
that refers to a heterogeneous group of disorders	"The disorders grouped under the learning disability label are thought to be specific and different in kind, i.e., they are 'heterogeneous' in nature. This phrase implies that the specific causes of the disorders are also many and dissimilar."
manifested by significant difficulties	"The effects of the disorders on an individual are detrimental to a consequential degree; that is, their presence handicaps and seriously limits the performance of some key ability. Because the NJCLD was concerned that 'learning-disabled' is often used as a synonym for 'mildly handicapped,' the Committee wanted to emphasize that the presence of learning disabilities in an individual can be as debilitating as the presence of cerebral palsy, mental defect, blindness or any handicapping condition."
in the acquisition and use of listening, speaking, reading, writing, reasoning or mathematical abilities.	"To be considered learning-disabled, an individual's disorder has to result in serious impairment of one or more of the listed abilities."
These disorders are intrinsic to the individual	"This phrase means that the source of the disorder is to be found within the person who is affected. The disability is not imposed on the individual as a consequence of economic deprivation, poor child-rearing practices, faulty school instruction, societal pressures, cultural differences, etc. Where present, such factors may complicate treatment, but they are not considered to be the cause of the learning disability."
and presumed to be due to central nervous system dysfunction.	"The cause of the learning disability is a known or presumed dysfunction in the central nervous system. Such dysfunctions may be by-products of traumatic damage to tissues, inherited factors, biochemical insufficiencies or imbalances, or other similar conditions that affect the central nervous system. The phrase is intended to spell out clearly the intent behind the statement that learning disabilities are intrinsic to the individual." (Hammill et al. 1981, p.339–340)

vironmental influences (*e.g.*, cultural differences, in-sufficient-inappropriate instruction, psychogenic factors), it is not the direct result of those conditions or influences. (Hammill, Leigh, McNutt. & Larsen, 1981, p.336).

To avoid further confusion arising from their definition, the group offered the detailed rationale that you see on the preceding page explaining specific aspects of the definition.

The definition and rationale suggested by the Association for Children and Adults with Learning Disabilities (ALCD) offered their own revision and rationale. (1985)

Specific Learning Disabilities is a chronic condition of presumed neurological origin which selec-tively interferes with the development, integration, and/or demonstration of verbal and/or nonverbal abilities. ...Specific Learning Disabilities exists as a distinct handicapping condition in the presence of average to superior intelligence, adequate sensory and motor systems, and adequate learning opportuni-ties. The condition varies in its manifestations and in degree of severity. ...Throughout life, the condition can affect self-esteem, education, vocation, social-ization and/or daily living activities.

Rationale of the ACLD Definition is below. Thus when we attempt to discuss learning-disabled students from a particular school district, we must exercise extreme caution in assuming their charac-teristics and generalizing ideas derived from ob-serving their behaviors. Instead, we must first es-

ALCD's Definition of Learning Disabilities

Specific Learning Disabilities	Specific Learning Disabilities (SLD) was selected to emphasize the fact that this condition has multiple manifestations but is **not** one of a generalized nature. Also, this is the term used in the Education of the Handicapped Act, the Education of All Handicapped Children Act, and the Rehabilitation Act of 1973, Section 504.
Condition	was made synonymous with SLD because it is a state of being. It is not merely a term nor does it affect only children, which some definitions suggest. For the first time the condition, not the population, is defined.
Chronic	was used to modify 'condition' to define its persistence in spite of the apparent waxing and waning of its manifestations.
Neurological origin	was inserted because early and recent authors of definitions have agreed to a central nervous system basis.
Presumed	was used to modify 'neurological origin' since there are not yet tools to determine origin definitively.
Interferes	is the active verb because the condition does not necessarily destroy or delete function but may variously impair, alter or redirect functions.
Selectively	was used to qualify the global concept of 'interferes' because the condition differentially affects abilities while leaving others unaffected.
Development, integration, and/or demonstration	this phrase was selected to denote the disruptions the condition creates in devel-oping and using intrinsic abilities
Verbal or non-verbal abilities	were chosen as inclusive terms to emphasize not only receptive and expressive language problems. but also the conceptual and thinking difficulties, the integrat-ing problems and motoric problems. This approach is more descriptive and desirable than the previous approach focusing primarily on verbal and academic manifestations.

ALCD's Definition of Learning Disabilities (continued)	
Distinct	signifies that SLD is separate and different from any other handicap and that any required interventions must be uniquely designed.
Handicapping	was used because the condition meets the definitional criteria contained in Section 504 of the Rehabilitation Act of 1973 and to emphasize possible eligibility for assistance under all federal legislation for persons with handicaps.
Intelligence	was inserted to avoid quantitative measurement terminology and to prevent direct translation into 'IQ scores.'
Average to superior	was included because the condition of Specific Learning Disabilities selectively interferes with abilities throughout the range of intelligence. Because of this selective interference, composite scores are inappropriate for use with SLD. Also, it is recognized that appropriate interventions can raise measured scores while a lack of or inappropriate interventions can lead to deterioration, not only on measured scores, but even of the individual.
Average– superior intelligence	was used to emphasize its co-existence and the potential need for services even among those with very high potential. The condition is not only of generalized low learning ability.
Adequate sensory and motor systems	was included to clarify the distinction of the condition from other known sensory and motor deficits.
Adequate learning opportunities	was selected to emphasize that the condition does **not arise** from a lack of exposure to life experiences and/or education typical to the community for the same age group.
Varies in its manifestations	was selected to emphasize that SLD does not equate with one or more functional deficits, e.g., reading disability, but is demonstrated in many signs and symptoms.
Varies	was used to denote its apparent changes in manifestation within the individual and to state that it is not identical across occurrences.
Degrees of severity	was inserted to clarify further the variance of the condition among the population and the variance in the extend to which it interferes with major life skills.
Throughout life	was used to emphasize that the condition persists into and throughout adulthood and it begins the sentence to connote its early presence.
Affect	was the preferred verb rather than disrupts, damages, impairs, interrupts, etc., because the condition may depreciate the function of some abilities while, simultaneously, the person may enhance other abilities through compensation.
Can	was used to modify the verb 'affect' to allow for differential effects on the areas to follow
Self-esteem, education, vo- cation socializa- tion, and/or daily living	were used to establish the potential influences of the condition not only on school achievement, but also on areas of life such as family life, community living, selection of competitive employment or even on learning how to drive a car.*

* Reproduction of this Definition is granted by ACLD with the provision that the Definition also be accompanied by the Rationale.

tablish our philosophical position on the nature of learning disabilities as well as giftedness and use our definitions as a foundation in formulating goals, expectations and teaching strategies to meet the needs of GLD students.

A Definition

For our purposes in defining GLD students, we find the ACLD definition (1985) particularly appropriate, especially their discussion of inclusion of the phrase, "average and superior intelligence," and their contention that the disability can affect adjustment throughout life. The following points, moreover, will add further clarity to our assumptions about the nature of learning disabilities especially important to our philosophical position and resulting educational strategies concerning students who are gifted and learning-disabled:

1. These students are able to learn and accumulate knowledge in ways not traditional in academic settings.
2. The disability is of a more permanent nature where compensation techniques are of primary importance.
3. The learning disability causes the individual to face frustration and failure in specific areas which require learning inputs, strategies or products which may be directly opposed to the individual's natural learning style. This in turn may cause failure and frustration for students. Results from these unsuccessful learning experiences are often manifested in disruptive behavior, poor self-efficacy, short attention span and hyperactivity. These characteristic behaviors are thought to interfere with learning. However, because they are often situation specific, we do not view them as causes, but in many instances, as effects. (Whitmore, 1980; Baum, 1984, 1988; Baum & Dixon, 1985; Dixon & Baum, 1986; Baum & Owen, 1988).

An Historical Perspective of Gifts and Talents

As is the case with learning disabilities, difficulty in establishing a unitary conception of giftedness still dominates the field. Beliefs range from very conservative and restrictive ideas as reflected in state definitions where giftedness is scoring in the ninety-seventh percentile or above on standardized intelligence tests, to extremely liberal, inclusive views that suggest that everyone has a special gift of worth to society (Taylor, 1986).

In order to gain an understanding of the existence of such huge differences in definition, we should trace briefly the development of the field. Throughout history, until the advent of intelligence testing and the IQ score, giftedness was equated with productivity. Indeed, early civilizations recognized as gifted those citizens who exhibited strong talents or potential in specific domains valuable to the individual culture. Leaders, orators, scientists, artists and great warriors were the gold of society. Efforts were made to identify youngsters showing early signs of talent in such areas and provide them with special training to develop this talent. During the Renaissance, these practices were repeated. Gifted individuals were highly valued. Patrons provided encouragement and financial support to struggling young talent recognized by their work or creative product. It was Mozart's performances that brought him attention by the court; the early works of Michelangelo likewise caught the eye of the de Medici family. School achievement and IQ scores were not the primary predictors of giftedness. Rather, it was superior performance and dedication that forecast future greatness.

However, today the stereotype of a gifted youngster conjures up the image of the straight-A student who boasts an IQ of at least 130. In some instances, test scores have taken precedence over actual performance. In fact we do know that more than a few of civilization's most gifted individuals, such as Newton, Edison and Churchill who did not do well in school might very well be excluded from gifted programs by today's standards.

This shift in emphasis began in the late nineteenth and early twentieth centuries when the movement toward testing and measuring predictors of success slowly replaced the evaluation of products as indicators of giftedness. Sir Francis Galton started this transition.

Influenced by his cousin, Charles Darwin, Galton was convinced that genius was an inherited trait and that intelligence was related to the keenness of one's senses. He thus argued that tests of sensory acuity could effectively measure intelligence or genius.

At the same time, but across the English Channel, two psychologists, Alfred Binet and his assistant, T. Simon, were commissioned by the French Ministry of Education to develop a test to identify children too dull to benefit from traditional schooling. After many unsuccessful attempts, they finally devised a scale based on specific skills that teachers felt students needed to achieve in school. They invented the concept of mental age to interpret test performance. The mental age concept eventually led to the first IQ or intelligence quotient. Although Binet warned against the overuse and sole reliance on a score to determine a child's capabilities, the realm of the all-powerful IQ score had begun.

Before long the idea swept across the Atlantic, finding further excitement and support by many. But most important to the field of giftedness was its effect on Lewis Terman. Terman, a professor at Stanford University, translated and refined Binet and Simon's work and in 1916 published the first form of the Stanford-Binet test of intelligence. From that time until the 1950's, giftedness was simply measured with an IQ test. Characteristics of gifted students were based on the landmark study undertaken by Terman and his associates (Terman, 1926; Burke, Jansen & Terman, 1930; Terman & Oden, 1947). They identified fourteen hundred students with an IQ score of at least 140 on the *Stanford-Binet Intelligence Test*, and conducted a comprehensive, longitudinal study on the personality characteristics and later creative accomplishments of these young geniuses. Early findings perpetuated the "Terman Myth": "that gifted students are only those who excel in all areas of endeavor and score high on any achievement and aptitude test" (Whitmore, 1980, p.13). Early signs of this discomfort began with Witty's (1958, p.62) assertion that "any child whose performance in a potentially valuable line of human activity is consistently remarkable" may be considered gifted. The movement continued with leaders voicing new ideas and opinions. Hildreth (1966) asserted that

> ...today the simple formula of 'giving a Binet' and deciding where to 'draw the line' no longer suffices. If giftedness is viewed as developed capacities and unusual performance in a wide range of skills and achievements, the identification of the gifted and talented requires a many-sided study of the individual's intellectual abilities. (p.147)

This shift of emphasis away from using a high IQ score as the sole indicator of giftedness was further supported by other research. Wallach (1976) found that test scores do not necessarily reflect the potential for creative productive accomplishments (Renzulli, 1978, p.182). Getzels and Jackson (1962) and Guilford (1962) pointed to the importance of creativity as an ability separate from intelligence and Guilford (1959) splintered intelligence into 120 separate skills. The necessity of including other areas of human endeavor eventually led to the revised adoption by the federal government in 1978 of the definition suggested by the Marland Report (1971):

> Children, and where applicable, youth, who are identified at the preschool, elementary, or secondary level as possessing demonstrated or potential abilities that give evidence of high performance capability in areas such as intellectual, creative, specific academic or leadership ability, or in the performing and visual arts, and who by reason thereof require services or activities not ordinarily provided by the school. (PL 95-561)

Although the federal definition allowed for a variety of superior abilities across specific fields, it failed to recognize non-intellective skills shown by many researchers to enhance creative production (Roe, 1953; Terman, 1959; MacKinnon, 1965). In essence, according to Renzulli (1986), what seemed to be emerging were two different kinds of giftedness—schoolhouse giftedness and creative-productive giftedness.

This distinction is essential in understanding students who can be learning-disabled and gifted at the same time. Schoolhouse giftedness defines students who are exceptional test-takers and talented lesson-learners. Their superior performance in school not only indicates high cognitive ability, but also their ability to learn in traditional ways—to work within the system. On the other hand, Renzulli explains that creative productive giftedness occurs when students use this knowledge and problem solving abilities to develop original products and ideas. These products often grow out of students' individual strengths and interests in areas of personal relevance.

Based on research on creative production, Renzulli (1978) provided a definition of creative-productive giftedness which emphasizes specific behavioral traits, both intellective and non-intellective. In his definition, giftedness or gifted behavior is viewed as the interaction among three clusters of traits: above-average ability, creativity, and task commitment that are brought to bear on **a specific area** of human endeavor (see figure below). For GLD students, we often find these traits in activities undertaken outside of the school setting where they are free to pursue interests in ways they learn best. These traits will be discussed more fully in Chapter 7 when we focus on identification of gifted behaviors in learning-disabled students.

In conclusion, it is important to restate the key points or assumptions we will use in discussing giftedness or gifted behavior within this book.

Giftedness
1. Is creative-productive in nature;
2. Occurs in certain individuals in *specific* areas at certain times;
3. Evidence for Renzulli's separate traits can be derived from any area of a student's life, in both positive or negative situations;
4. Task commitment is not synonymous with attention span, high achievement in all academic areas and homework done consistently

well. Rather it represents "the capacity for high levels of interest, enthusiasm, fascination and involvement in a particular problem area of study or form of human expression (Renzulli & Reis, 1985).

In summary, we see that early definitions of genius or giftedness involved creative production. However, as theorists became fixated on IQ, definitions drifted away form actual performance to test scores. Today however, a return to the earlier notion seems apparent. Aside from Renzulli's emphasis on creative production, others recommend looking at superior performances in specific areas. Gardner (1983) posits that there are multiple intelligences or areas of talents where individuals can excel. Tannenbaum (1983) argues that gifts are identified by teaching specific skills in specific domains and evaluating resulting performance. These broadened conceptions of giftedness help us to avoid considering giftedness as extraordinary productivity in all areas. More important, they allow us greater flexibility in identifying and justifying the existence of specific gifts and talents among LD students.

GRAPHIC REPRESENTATION OF THE THREE-RING DEFINITION OF GIFTEDNESS

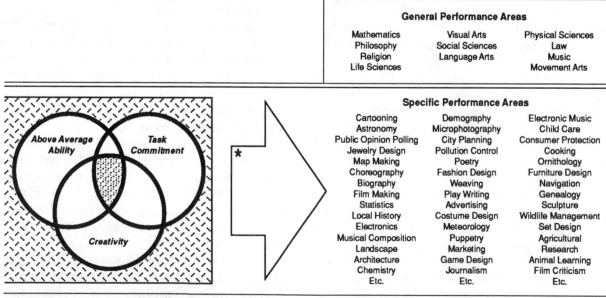

* This arrow should be read as ". . . brought to bear upon . . ."

CHAPTER 3

LEARNING-DISABLED AND GIFTED: WHO ARE THEY?

Who, then, is the student who is both gifted and learning-disabled? Simply spoken, the gifted, LD student is a child who exhibits remarkable talents or strengths in some areas and disabling weaknesses in others. These students can be found in three general varieties.

The Three Varieties of GLD Students

Identified Gifted Students Who Have Subtle Learning Disabilities

First consider the students whom everyone knows are gifted. These students are first noticed for their achievement. High IQ scores and high grades place these youngsters in programs for the gifted. However, for some of them, discrepancies appear between expected and actual performance. These students may charm with verbal talent while their spelling or handwriting contradicts this image. At times these all-knowing students are forgetful, sloppy and disorganized. As they reach middle school and junior high years where there is more long-term written work and heavier emphasis on comprehensive, independent reading, some bright students find it increasingly difficult to achieve. Like Neil, they may become depressed and confused about why a gifted youngster should experience such difficulty.

Because below grade level achievement is the usual signal for a psycho-educational screening for possible learning disabilities, these unfortunate bright students are often passed over. A "C" average to many school personnel is no reason to refer a student for testing even though that same student demonstrates a well-above-average learning potential. The identification of a subtle learning disability would help the student understand his situation. More importantly, professionals could offer learning strategies and compensation techniques to help these learning-disabled gifted students deal with the duality of learning behaviors.

A word of caution is necessary at this point. Because gifted students are not achieving up to their potential does not guarantee that they are learning-disabled. There are other reasons why bright students may not be meeting academic expectations. Perhaps expectations are unrealistic. Excelling in science, for example, is no assurance that high level performance will also be found in other areas. Motivation, interest and specific aptitudes influence the amount of effort students apply to a task and the quality of performance. In other instances, the student's self-expectations are so high that a task is never—and cannot be—finished to perfection. As the student becomes dimly aware of the struggle between perfectionism and impossibility, procrastination may be an escape route, although that leads to other conflicts.

Underachievement also may result when the student perceives the curriculum to be unchallenging or irrelevant. Some bright students do not subscribe to the school's value system. Sometimes, for example, grades are trivial, and these bright youngsters search out other rewards in other environments.

Possibly the curriculum had been so beneath student ability in the elementary grades that these students never learned how to study or apply themselves when assignments require more memory, organization and planning. It is essential to rule out these explanations before assuming a learning disability is present. In essence, one must ask whether the behavior is indicative of a learning disability or simply indicative of other curricular-related issues.

Unidentified Students

The second group of youngsters in which this combination of learning behaviors may be found are those identified as neither gifted nor learning-disabled. These are students whose learning disability has been masked by their high intellectual ability. This ability enables these bright youngsters to compensate sufficiently to perform at grade level. In essence, their intellectual ability hides the disability and the disability disguises the gift. These students are difficult to find since they do not flag our attention by exceptional behaviors. Often the talents of these hidden gifted emerge in specific content areas or with a teacher who uses a more creative approach in the classroom. Sometimes a talent emerges in particular learning environments where written production is minimized in favor of projects, drama, debate and discussion and where nontraditional teaching methods are common.

Identified Learning-Disabled Students Who Are Also Gifted

The third group consists of students who are discovered within the identified learning-disabled population. Unlike the GLD students with a subtle learning disability, these bright children are often failing in school. They are first noticed by school personnel for what they *cannot* do. This group of students is most at risk because of the implicit message that accompanies the LD label: You are broken. Bright and sensitive GLD students respond to the emphasis placed on their disability with genuine feelings of inadequacy. This feeling overshadows any positive feelings connected with their special gift or talent. Unfortunately, the system reinforces these negative, pessimistic attitudes. Until they are fixed and made normal again, little attention is given to their gift or talent. This practice values acquisition of basic skills over creative productive behavior. Clearly, skills in reading, spelling and writing take preference over a child's talent in building bridges, or the gift of using art to explain conflict, or a child's commitment to save the whale by starting a city-wide campaign. If the gift is noticed, it may be misused or abused, as evidenced by the case of Neil and his photography.

The prevalence of potential giftedness among this population is higher than we might expect and is often related to how school districts identify their learning-disabled populations. In a study examining the traits of high ability learning-disabled students (Baum, 1985), as many as thirty-three percent of an identified LD population also had superior intellectual ability.

Table 3.1 lists the percentage of identified LD students in grades four–six from six New England districts who attained an IQ score of at least 120 on the verbal or performance scales of the *WISC*. A score of 120 falls within the superior range of

Table 3.1   Percentage of LD Students with Superior Abilities

District	*% of LD Population with High IQ*
District A	25
District B	6
District C	6
District D	20
District E	19
District F	33

intelligence (Wechsler, 1974) and is claimed as a minimum threshold for high level of creativity (Guilford, 1967).

An odd finding was the extreme reluctance of parents of bright LD students to allow their children to participate in the study. No similar problems existed with the parents of gifted students or learning-disabled students with average ability. This unwillingness suggests that parents of high ability LD students are troubled and frustrated by current practices and procedures. In fact, in newer programs specifically designed for this population, parents expressed relief and gratitude that the gifts of the children were finally recognized and reinforced (Dixon & Baum, 1986).

To summarize, GLD children have well-above-average ability in specific areas, show a creative approach in specific situations and are committed to some interest or real world problem. In addition, they are not performing in certain academic areas due to identified deficits in learning processes.

Table 3.2 summarizes these indicators for the three students discussed in Chapter 1.

Characteristics of Gifted, Learning-Disabled Students

Viewed broadly, two sets of strategies exist in special education today. They are designed either to remediate weaknesses or to develop superior abilities. To understand how these strategies may be used with students who are both gifted and learning-disabled, we will explore cognitive and affective characteristics these students bring to the learning situation. Although only a few studies have examined these students, we are able to draw from them to paint a clear picture of the learning characteristics of this population. The most important characteristics of GLD students are specific cognitive abilities, creative tendencies, self-concept, motivation, and behavior.

Table 3.2   Sample Indicators of Giftedness and Learning Disabilities

| Name | Above-Average Ability | | Creativity | Task Commitment | LD Problem |
	General	Specific			
Neil	120 IQ	Photography photo won first prize	Class Clown, Photographic essay, values	Taught self to play piano and guitar	Difficulty in remembering sequences in math and organizing thought in written work
Jimmy	134 IQ	Mechanical abilities, could take things apart, explain how they work	Excuses for avoiding tasks, compensation strategies developed on own to bypass weaknesses (used drawing to take notes)	Worked on survey even when tedious and boring because he felt it was important	Difficulty in reading and writing despite superior scores in verbal and performance areas of WISC-R.
Debby	128 IQ	Drama, Interests in world	Great ideas in brainstorming activities. Original ideas in architectural design with Legos™	Wrote letter to President Reagan to protest nuclear war (Even though she hated writing and could not spell). Time spent on "A Day in the Life of Jerusha Webster" project.	Poor self-concept. Limited reading and writing ability. Overdependence on adults.

Intellectual Skills

Most studies examining cognitive abilities of GLD students are based on patterns derived from the *Wechsler Intelligence Scale for Children—Revised* (Wechsler, 1974). These studies have examined the possibility that certain intellectual patterns distinguish GLD students as a group. The results of three major research efforts give insight into the learning patterns of GLD students.

Fox and her colleagues at Johns Hopkins University (1983) studied the WISC-R profiles of 450 GLD students between the ages of six and fifteen with reading problems. Giftedness was defined by scores of at least 125 on either the performance or verbal scale of the WISC-R. Documentation of the presence of a learning disability was provided by case history information, observations of behavior, reading achievement of at least two years below grade level, and evidence of a significant discrepancy between intellectual potential and academic performance. The researchers then organized subtest scores according to Bannatyne's (1974) recategorization of the WISC subscales. The four categories—acquired knowledge, spatial, conceptual, and sequencing—are composed of three subtests, each shown below. Fox and her coworkers found that gifted LD students with reading problems perform best on conceptual and spatial tasks and worst on tasks requiring memorization of isolated facts and sequencing.

A second study (Schiff, Kaufman, & Kaufman, 1981), examining clusters of ability among GLD children, found slightly different results. The thirty students in the study, ages nine to sixteen, were selected from a private clinic. Giftedness was shown with a score above 120 on either the performance or verbal scales of the WISC-R. These students also showed a significant difference between intelligence and achievement in some academic area. (This deficit area did not need to be below-grade level, however.) Finally, these students displayed many behavioral traits associated with learning disabilities such as hyperactivity and poor visual-motor or gross-motor skills. For most of these youngsters, their parents—not their schools—had requested special testing.

In this study, verbal conceptualization and acquired knowledge subtests were strong areas and spatial and sequencing abilities were weaker. The difference between the Fox and Schiff studies may be attributed to two causes. First, the populations of the two studies were different. Fox's study dealt with students whose reading abilities were two years below grade level; Schiff's study did not isolate reading problems or below-grade-level performance. Second, students in the Schiff study were performing at or above grade level, suggesting that they had found success in both verbal conceptualization and acquired knowledge areas. Both studies confirm, however, that GLD students are able to conceptualize and think at abstract levels. It is their poor memory for isolated facts and deficient organizational abilities that interfere with school performances.

The third study is the work we have been conducting over the past several years investigating gifted students from identified learning-disabled populations (ages nine to thirteen). Giftedness is documented by observations of extraordinary performance in activities requiring problem solving, creative production in areas associated

---

Bannatyne Recategorization of WISC (1974)

1. Acquired knowledge = Information +Arithmetic +Vocabulary

2. Spatial = Picture completion +Block design +Object assembly

3. Conceptual = Comprehension + Similarities + Vocabulary

4. Sequencing = Digit Span + Arithmetic + Coding

with visual literacy, drama, or spatial design. Once giftedness is documented, WISC-R profiles are analyzed for specific cognitive patterns. Strengths are seen in similarities, block design, comprehension, picture arrangement, and object assembly. Vocabulary and information are often found as secondary strengths. Typical weaknesses are shown in digit span, arithmetic, and coding. These results have led us to theorize about the role of an integrative intelligence and its effect on learning and achievement with GLD children. Chapter Six is devoted to a discussion of Integrative Intelligence and its educational implications.

To conclude, it appears that GLD students demonstrate superior abilities in forming concepts and manipulating abstract ideas. For them, successful learning experiences depend on meaningful interactions with subject matter. Isolated details that are not an important part of a "bigger picture" are not assimilated. Although the minds of these students may be filled with broad, grandiose ideas and abstract concepts, they often cannot express them through organized written products because of difficulties in sequencing and lack of attention to detail. Education for these children must focus on abstract ideas and generalization. Teachers must provide organizational strategies to help these students achieve and allow alternatives to writing as a means of communication. These ideas will be discussed more fully in the subsequent chapters.

Behavior

Other studies concentrate on motivation, behavior, self-concept, and creative tendencies in bright learning-disabled students (Baum, 1985; Whitmore, 1981; Schiff *et al.*, 1981). The results of three studies will be examined to provide a more complete picture of the typical GLD student. All these studies show that, although GLD youngsters demonstrate superior abilities in certain areas and have often completed impressive creative feats (winning at science fairs, breeding ants and tropical fish, producing a record, etc.), they tend to be unhappy and frustrated with themselves.

Schiff *et al.* (1981) conducted intensive interviews with the thirty GLD students and their parents. He reported that these students were emotionally upset and generally unhappy because of their frustrations in activities requiring motor coordina-

tion and organizational abilities (for example, physical education, spelling, math computation). They felt powerless and vengeful. Schiff remarked that the emotional behaviors of these children were more severe and more troublesome than expected.

These findings were confirmed by Whitmore (1981) in her work with young gifted underachievers. Whitmore studied the emotional, behavioral, creative characteristics of underachieving six- to eight-year-olds, most of whom could be classified as hyperactive or learning disabled. As in Schiff's study, she found contradictions on achievement, motivation, and feelings of worth. While in school the children were often aggressive, disruptive, and off-task. Their completed work tended to be sloppy and suggested weak effort. But in nonacademic settings these same students put forth sustained effort toward their own hobbies and interests. Whitmore found that these students were active problem solvers, analytic thinkers, and showed strong task commitment and effort when the topic was meaningful.

Schiff's and Whitmore's conclusions were based on observation and interviews. Baum (1985) tested and extended these findings with more comprehensive measures. One hundred twelve gifted or learning-disabled students in grades four through six participated in the study. These students were classified into three groups based on their intelligence: Superior, LD-Superior, and LD-Average. Students in the Superior group were classified as gifted by their local school district based on a discrepancy formula and had an IQ score of at least 120 on the Performance or Verbal Scales of the WISC-R. LD-Superior students were classified as learning-disabled by their local school district and had an IQ score of at least 120 on the Performance or Verbal Scales of the WISC-R. The LD-Average group were identified as learning-disabled by their local school district and had a Full Scale IQ of at least 90, but not exceeding a score of 119 on the Verbal or Performance Scales of the WISC-R. A variety of instruments was used to assess and compare cognitive and motivational behavior patterns in the three groups.

From the battery of tests, the group profiles were compared. The findings of this analysis indicated that three groups are distinguishable. As might be expected, the superior non-disabled students are plainly different from both learning-disabled popu-

Table 3.3   Group Means and Standard Deviations for 24 Predictor Variables

Variable	Group					
	LD-Average		LD-Superior		Superior	
	M	SD	M	SD	M	SD
Self-Efficacy for Academic Tasks						
Perceived success	16.09	8.19	15.55	7.19	24.39	5.82
Perceived failure	4.47	4.04	5.73	4.56	1.00	1.44
Perceived school skills	11.63	11.24	9.89	10.28	23.38	6.72
Overall academic self-efficacy	78.81	11.12	78.00	10.10	91.19	6.77
Creative Potential						
Self-perception of creative traits	20.74	4.15	22.64	3.71	23.50	4.06
Teacher perception of creativity	20.43	11.40	33.37	17.63	56.35	!6.31
Figural divergent thinking	108.75	12.83	110.50	12.35	114.12	12.04
Verbal originality	94.90	15.11	100.17	15.03	108.91	14.62
Figural originality	112.18	23.98	111.04	24.29	116.27	20.57
Creative interests	22.58	14.36	26.62	6.2	22.20	9.11
Spatial interests	.39	.49	.65	.48	.43	.49
Disruptive Behavior						
Teacher perception of disruptive behavior	12.43	8.00	14.33	11.93	5.15	6.28
Self-Concept						
Self-concept	51.58	9.15	50.60	9.27	57.38	6.51
Locus of Control						
Internal control for success	13.47	3.97	12.27	2.61	13.68	1.84
Internal control for failure	10.38	3.43	9.34	3.53	11.00	2.26

Table 3.3 (Continued)

Variable	Group					
	LD-Average		LD-Superior		Superior	
	M	SD	M	SD	M	SD
Attribution for Academic Success and Failure						
Success attributed to ability	29.08	26.79	23.17	23.90	30.53	24.66
Success attributed to effort	32.38	21.25	41.34	29.08	31.44	17.02
Success attrib. to task difficulty	28.42	24.54	37.09	29.26	36.66	23.90
Success attributed to luck	7.16	8.47	3.83	5.68	1.91	4.49
Failure attributed to lack of ability	4.62	10.53	1.70	4.99	4.93	16.31
Failure attributed to lack of effort	28.65	29.28	24.74	31.44	17.31	30.96
Failure attributed to task difficulty	21.12	32.99	32.99	39.42	15.00	29.95
Failure attributed to bad luck	6.36	9.82	10.71	24.64	4.95	16.85
Failure attributed to shyness	13.94	24.16	25.82	39.63	3.21	10.15

lations. Accounting for most of the difference is teachers' perceptions of student creativity. Teachers rated the superior students much higher on creative traits than they rated both groups of learning-disabled youngsters. Understandably, the gifted students also felt best about their ability to do well on academic tasks (academic self-efficacy). The LD-Superior students are viewed as more creative and report higher levels of interest in creative extracurricular activities than do their LD-Average peers, but they are more disruptive and frustrated in school. LD-Superior youngsters think that school offers plenty of occasions for failure, and they often ascribe their academic failures to shyness.

In short, LD-Superior students show high levels of creative potential coupled with low levels of academic success and a tendency toward disruptive behavior. This curious profile invites misbehavior and frustration. The major factors distin-

guishing LD-Superiors from both other groups is a heightened sense of inadequacy in school. In contrast to superior students, LD-Superiors experience fewer school successes and considerably more failures. Even compared with less able learning-disabled students, the LD-Superior group perceived themselves as failing more frequently in school. Why bright LD students have such a poor sense of efficacy when they possess greater intellectual and creative potential will be discussed in Part Two. Table 3.3 shows means and standard deviations for each of the three groups on the variables studied.

In summary, GLD students have learning and motivational patterns different from those of their peers. In Part Two of this book we examine these patterns more closely to discover what implications they have for designing educational experiences for these special students.

PART TWO

Theoretical Perspectives

INTRODUCTION

In Part One we explored the unique characteristics of students who are both learning-disabled and gifted. We also offered a rationale for developing special programs for these youngsters to aim them toward their intellectual and creative potential.

Before we can suggest specific ideas or strategies to use with gifted, learning-disabled students, however, it is essential to consider how they learn and why particular learning strategies are sometimes successful and sometimes not. Incorporated in this discussion are contemporary theories of motivation, learning, and intelligence. These theories form the necessary foundation for developing successful learning experiences.

GLD students frequently appear unmotivated and off-task on school-related assignments but can focus and complete projects of a more complex nature at home. In Chapter 4 we use several theories of motivation to explain these paradoxical behaviors. The first theory discussed is the role of arousal and sensory stimulation and how particular methods of arousal seem to have positive effects with GLD students. A particularly relevant aspect of this theory is its application to the ongoing debate on the cause of a GLD student's hyperactive or inattentive behavior. We try to shed some light on whether off-task behavior is the result of an attention deficit disorder or simply a mismatch of curriculum with the student's intellectual abilities and learning styles. A second theory explains the role of self-efficacy (the perception of competence) in academic success. Several suggestions are given for enhancing academic self-efficacy in students. The final motivational theory described is attributions for success and failure. This theory of how students view the causes and consequences of their behavior is useful in understanding frequent behaviors exhibited by GLD students such as task avoidance and misunderstanding of the role of effort.

Another area of concern when dealing with GLD students is their inability to use efficient learning strategies, especially when the task requires memory of unrelated facts or the organization of ideas, projects, or time. In Chapter 5 we summarize the current views of cognitive learning researchers who describe effective self-regulating strategies that effective learners use. Through further examples we show why learning disabled students have difficulty in completing certain tasks, but, when interested, can compensate successfully. Additionally, we emphasize the role teachers must play in helping GLD students to identify and to practice specific cognitive strategies necessary for academic success.

A third area important in planning programs for these students is the appropriate use of diagnostic information gained through typical assessment procedures. Because the *Wechsler Intelligence Scale for Children-Revised* is the most common measure given to identify GLD students, its use in estimating intellectual strengths of these students is in Chapter 6. A Discussion of two intellectual patterns—Dispersive and Integrative—provides an understanding about why GLD students tend to have inconsistent learning behaviors. The second part of this chapter presents two case studies to show how to interpret the WISC-R profiles to provide appropriate programs to nurture these students' gifts. For it is through their gifts that these students will discover how they learn best and what strategies it takes to achieve success. Finally, we show through case studies how awareness of self-regulated learning strategies can help students to generalize these strategies to more difficult tasks.

CHAPTER 4

MOTIVATION

In the first part of this book we discussed the motivational patterns of the GLD child. At home, these students are highly motivated to tackle innovative and complex tasks. At school it is a different and perplexing story. When assignments are completed—and frequently they are not—the work lacks effort and precision. Another relevant characteristic is the difficulty many learning-disabled students have when they are asked to pay attention to a particular task. We suspect that the difficulty stems not so much from the inability to attend but from an environment insensitive to the youngster's strengths and needs. Lastly, GLD pupils may set unreasonably high standards for themselves; when they cannot reach the mark, they view themselves as failures. Eventually, these expectations settle into task avoidance and feelings of helplessness.

In this chapter we examine several approaches to motivation that will be useful in understanding the classroom behavior of the learning-disabled student. We offer a few practical suggestions and expand them in Chapter 9.

What is Motivation?

Twenty minutes into the lesson, you become aware of two boys in the back of the room who appear to be paying no attention to your carefully prepared lecture. One is staring out the window; the other is scribbling and squirming. Have you bored them already? Do they not want to learn? What do you do now? These questions and their answers concern motivation in the classroom, a topic that itself has motivated much research and generated a lot of theory, but little agreement. So before we discuss what to do about inattentive pupils like these two boys, let us consider some theoretical points about motivation.

In approaching the topic of motivation, the first step is to determine what motivation is. That sounds easy enough. Almost any teacher will assert that a motivated student is one who enthusiastically tries to master whatever the teacher wants the student to learn. Thus an unmotivated student is one who does not enthusiastically engage in learning, and who, indeed, may actively and enthusiastically *avoid* learning.

That seems to say it. But before we go further, we know that psychologists will want to add their two dollars worth. Although their definitions vary, most theorists think that motivation embodies two components: *energy* and *direction*. So theories of motivation try to explain what energized behavior in the direction of some goal. Why do people, including students, behave in certain ways, persist in those ways, and change their ways?

The teachers' consensus, then, that eager students are motivated and unreceptive students are unmotivated is far off base. Both kinds of students are motivated, one kind to achieve a goal that requires study and the other kind to avoid study. The second kind may manifest motivation in a number of ways: by remaining passive, by actively resisting, by distracting the attention of the class, by being disruptive, to cite only a few.

Because motivation sprawls across most human behavior, most theorists have found it useful to discuss more specific portions of motivation. In fact, there are now so many theories about motivation's sub-parts that it would take a couple of books to survey them. We will consider instead a few of the more recent, better-researched aspects.

Arousal and Sensory Stimulation

There is considerable evidence that all organisms require stimulation to survive. Stimulation of the sensory apparatus—hearing, sight, touch, taste—serves to arouse the organism. Arousal is not all there is to motivation, of course. We must blend in some sense of direction. Arousal is an essential beginning; it sets the stage for goal-directed behavior.

The scientific credibility of this idea was strengthened back in the mid-1950's when McGill University students volunteered to enter an environment in which they would do nothing but lie on a cot. (They had short breaks to eat and use the bathroom.) They were fitted with translucent goggles to dim vision, cuffs on the hands and arms to impede the sense of touch, and earphones that delivered constant "white noise." They earned twenty dollars a day, a hefty allowance at the time, but few students could take more than a couple of days of the experiment. They reported unmanageable stress, extreme boredom, hallucinations, and mental dullness, among other unpleasant effects. These findings suggested that sensory deprivation is unhealthy, or reversing the principle, that humans have an inborn need for arousal.

Combined with other research, the McGill experiments help to confirm an important principle of arousal. It is summarized by the well-known inverted U curve shown in Figure 4.1. Too little stimulation, as happened in the deprivation studies, impairs learning and performance. Too much stimulation works the same way. Studies of people whose jobs are chronically overstimulating, such as over-worked airport controllers, show unhappy outcomes: easy distraction, errors and degraded performance, ulcers, insomnia, nightmares, headaches, colitis, asthma, hypertension (Baldwin & Baldwin, 1981). The moral sounds simple: Moder-ate stimulation produces optimum attention and performance.

Unfortunately, it is not easy to translate that moral into classroom practice, because different students have different optimum arousal points. Some students, for example, have low arousability and require considerable stimulation. Others are aroused by low levels of stimulation (Farley, 1986). Such wide individual differences offer a stiff challenge for teachers trying to accommodate twenty youngsters simultaneously to assure optimum attention and alertness. Plans for classroom activities that are optimally stimulating will probably bore one student while thrilling another. The solution is to aim for a Golden Mean: Arrange activities that will be arousing for the majority, and offer enough variety so that each student will be optimally aroused at least some of the time. Here are a few things that can be varied without too much difficulty:

- Type of activity
- Amount of student participation
- Tempo or pace
- Amount of structure
- Domain stressed (cognitive, affective, psychomotor)
- Formality versus informality
- Stimulus complexity
- Style of feedback
- Cooperative or competitive activities
- Form of reinforcer

Because arousal is essential, people are motivated to behave in ways that gain optimum arousal. If the classroom environment provides too little

Figure 4.1   The Inverted U-Curve of Arousal

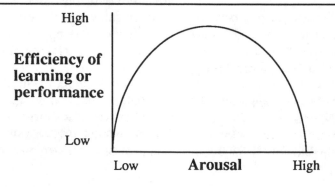

stimulation, students will invent their own means of arousal. When that happens, students are motivated toward goals that probably differ from classroom objectives. That is usually called misbehavior. Although misbehavior has many sources, effective teachers will reduce optional routes to arousal by heightening interest in lessons. This means focusing on student strengths and interests. When students are optimally aroused, learning, enjoyment, and a sense of efficacy comes naturally.

We have seen dramatic changes in attitudes, enthusiasm, behavior, and quality of work when students are encouraged to explain what they have learned in *their* preferred mode. For example, a group of fifth graders had been studying colonial American history. One learning objective was that students would be able to compare and contrast growing up in colonial times and today. We first asked the students to write a brief essay on the topic. The best essays, predictably, came from the best writers. Next, we repeated the assignment with a twist: The students could choose optional ways of communicating their learning—drama, drawing, building, even writing. This time, ninety percent of the projects were superior. The finished products were neat, organized, and sophisticated. Effort, arousal, and time on task had improved. The students were also enthusiastic and pleased with their accomplishments. The products of the learning-disabled youngsters were indistinguishable from the other students.

Arousal and Hyperactivity

One of the chief complaints about behavior disordered youngsters is that they fidget constantly, pay no attention to what is being taught, and have difficulty following instructions. Many of these students—mostly boys— are tagged with the important-sounding label, "attention deficit disorder: with hyperactivity" (American Psychiatric Association, 1987). Although learning disabilities are thought to be different from hyperactivity, Zukow (1975) estimates that learning disabilities *result from* hyperactivity in about seventy-five percent of hyperactive children.

Despite public outcry over the past decade, the preferred method of managing hyperactive youth is medication, usually stimulant drugs such as Ritalin. The drugs are claimed to have a "paradox-ical" effect, because when they work, children are calmer and more attentive. A different explanation is offered by Clarizio and McCoy (1984): Hyperactive people seem to have an "underpowered" portion of their brain that regulates arousal; they thus are much more active in seeking sensations from their environment. In this theory, stimulant medication does not have a paradoxical effect. It simply provides internal stimulation so that the child does not need to squeeze every drop of stimulation from the environment.

What causes hyperactivity? Certainly there is a genetic component (Ross & Ross, 1982), but there is also evidence that the environment makes a contribution. For example, a twenty-five-year-old longitudinal study showed that hyperactive teenagers improved notably when they left school (Borland & Heckman, 1976). The school environment is very clear about its demands: students should be docile, neat, quiet for extended periods, and interested in what the teacher is interested in.

Kids who need more stimulation are automatically at odds with these expectations. And the GLD student with hyperactivity stands in double jeopardy. On the gifted side, the child has an intrinsic urge to discover, understand, and master, and prefers active engagement in learning. On the LD side, when a school subject is mysteriously frustrating or not meaningful, the student may dodge that aversion by searching for optimal arousal elsewhere. When the classroom is highly structured and students must be passive for much of the school day, the GLD child is almost certain to show higher levels of activity than is acceptable. In her study of upper elementary GLD children, that is exactly what Baum (1985) found. Those children, she discovered, were characterized by feelings of inefficacy in academic behaviors. Their sense of scholarly ineptness probably increased motivation to avoid the usual school tasks, and the predictable result was disruptive classroom behavior.

Self-Efficacy

Albert Bandura (1986) defines self-efficacy as a person's belief that he can organize and carry out some behavior. As simple as it seems, self-efficacy is now claimed to have a central role in motivating human behavior. Compared to those with weak self-efficacy, people with a robust sense of efficacy spend more energy at a task, persevere longer, set more challenging goals, and persist in the face of barriers and occasional failure. Success thus becomes more likely for them, which in turn boosts self-efficacy.

Bandura's (1977) original work in self-efficacy focused on helping adults to overcome phobic behaviors such as fear of snakes. Later research has broadened to include a wide variety of ordinary behaviors in ordinary situations. For example, teacher and student self-efficacy have been shown to be powerful predictors of good instructions, positive attitudes, and student accomplishment (Ashton & Webb, 1986; Owen & Froman, 1988).

Efficacy expectations seem to span all three domains of human behavior. On the cognitive side of self-efficacy, a person must consider a goal, imagine working toward that goal, and make a prediction about success. The affective side is a poorly understood dimension ranging from reluctance, shyness, and anxiety about performance to exuberance, enthusiasm, and confidence. Self-efficacy is thus a reciprocal mix of cognitions about performances, plus a motivating torque of confidence. Such confidence spurs a person to try behaviors and improves the odds for success. As a person succeeds, self-efficacy is reinforced, and the heightened self-efficacy increases motivation to pursue similar tasks. The opposite also holds. For example, it is easy to predict that a student accustomed to failure will have low academic self-efficacy, and that perception will motivate him to avoid classroom goals.

How Does Efficacy Information Get Into the Head?

As we have implied, successful actions are the strongest forerunners to self-efficacy. A second influence is imitation learning. Respected models demonstrating skilled performances deliver cognitive information about how to carry out a task. They also vicariously instill efficacy information. This does not suggest that models should always demonstrate effortless performance in front of observers. Models who often succeed and occasionally struggle give two important messages: sometimes failures happen, and I can still have robust self-efficacy. Effective models may also be symbolic,

as plausible heroes in novels. Implausible models, as from commercial television, are imitated mainly when their behaviors are within reach of observers. These behaviors are ordinarily modest—trademark phrases, dress, gestures. Incredible behaviors—winning fist fights every ten minutes, arguing fluidly and persuasively no matter how silly the cause—have little imitative importance no matter how much the model is reinforced. That a few folks *do* try to copy astonishing behaviors testifies to their innocence; after a few ineffectual trials, they come to understand that their environment is not as supportive as the ones shown on TV.

Verbal persuasion is a third influence on self-efficacy. Teachers, preachers, parents, and peers spend much of their professional lives trying to persuade listeners to exhibit certain behaviors. Pleading, exhortation, and rational arguments become powerful only when they are coupled with successful performances. When a failing student is advised to follow a strict regimen of homework and study, but finds immediately that it is hard work and slacks off (fails), he chalks up one more example of free advice. So verbal persuasion is most effective when the talker can arrange the environment so that success is highly probable.

Finally, physiological signs of arousal alter self-efficacy. When, for example, a student experiences severe test anxiety, performance falters and the student quickly comes to expect that anxiety will accompany the next test. If that prediction comes true, anxiety becomes more tightly tied to test-taking behaviors, and will probably spread to associated activities such as studying and attending class. As anxiety increases, effective effort wanes, failure becomes more likely, and self-efficacy about academic performance dwindles.

There are abundant practical applications of self-efficacy theory. Teachers should consider, for example, how to assure success experiences, especially in classes of mixed ability students. Teachers may want to rethink their role as model, even when student imitation seems unlikely (as with adolescents), and they will want to know how to assess students' self-efficacy quickly and easily. Students with bloated confidence will make poor estimates of task demands and effort needed, and they are likely to engender failure. Those whose confidence is beneath their competence will lack endurance in school tasks and may even avoid them.

Enhancing Self-Efficacy

It is important to remember that GLD students have high standards for success. Acceptable performance in a watered-down curriculum will probably not be considered success. We repeatedly hear these students appeal for material at their grade level and for help so they can achieve the same quality of work as their gifted peers. With these principles in mind, we offer several specific suggestions that will help in boosting self-efficacy by increasing perceived success.

1. Carve big tasks into smaller pieces to increase the likelihood of success. Use more frequent evaluations of progress, rather than a couple of massive ones.

2. For genuine progress, hand out reinforcers liberally. Consider public reinforcers as well as private ones. Praise—public and private—is an inexpensive, natural reinforcer, and it can be extremely powerful. Ken Blanchard (co-author of *The One Minute Manager*) remarks that praise needs to be dished out about four times as frequently as criticism. Why? Studies with adults show that even when praise is twice as frequent as criticism, morale is weak. If adults need the four-to-one rule, why be stingy with kids? But keep reading...

3. Be careful using praise as a reinforcer. Beginning teachers have probably heard about the importance of praise in every course they have taken, but they often use it so carelessly that it loses effectiveness. Here are some guidelines about effective praise (Adapted from Brophy, 1981):

   • It is not delivered randomly or unsystematically.
   • It shows spontaneity, variety, and other signs of credibility.
   • It rewards attainment of specific performances (including effort).
   • It gives information about competence and the value of performance.
   • It uses past performance as the context for describing present performance.
   • It recognizes noteworthy effort or success at difficult tasks.
   • It attributes success to effort and ability, implying that similar successes can be expected in the future.

4. Remember that occasional failure may be challenging to the student with strong self-efficacy, but discouraging to the learner with feeble self-efficacy. You may have to invent ways of minimizing failure for students with low expectations. As you raise their expectations, they become more tolerant of obstacles and barriers.

5. Try to make tasks meaningful. Use events and illustrations that are important to the learner. Build new learning on what has already been learned. This can be extremely difficult when it is time to begin a new lesson and some students are nowhere close to mastering the previous one. But if your lessons are hierarchical—that is, if new content builds on previous work—and the student is not ready to move forward, failure will loom no matter how cleverly you present the material. When the youngster believes that new and valued content is within grasp, he will perceive learning as a reasonable and worthwhile challenge.

6. Use peer tutoring, especially with new learning. Peers usually act like coping models (who succeed, but with effort), and coping models are frequently more influential than mastery models (who show effortless performance).

7. Communicate expectations clearly. Tell learners exactly what you want accomplished (using instructional objectives), and accompany it with positive expectations.

8. Beware of accidentally communicating negative expectations. Good and Brophy (1987, pp. 128-129) summarize seventeen unintentional teacher behaviors that offer hidden lessons. Examples: less eye contact with low achievers; giving high achievers (but not lows) the benefit of the doubt in grading written work; calling on low achievers less often to answer questions.

9. Use more cooperative activities; try to lessen possible harmful effects from competition.

10. Reduce the possible aversion to time on task. Here are some typical aversive events for students. Each of them, with practice, can be altered.
    • Too few reinforcers and too many criticisms available
    • being pressured to move too quickly with difficult material

---

A practical example of stirring criterion-referenced measurement into a traditional classroom recipe. (Robert Slavin)

Calculate baseline scores for each student by finding the average percent correct form past quizzes and tests. (Or, at the beginning of the year, use last year's average.) For each quiz, compare the student's score with his baseline, and award improvement points thus:

5 or more points below baseline	=	0 improvement points
-4 to +4 points	=	1 improvement points
+5 to +9 points	=	2 improvement points
+10, up to a perfect score	=	3 improvement points

- being offered too much material at once
- being ignored or dodged after requesting help
- taking poorly written tests
- being told to stop an attractive (and worthwhile) activity
- not being able to distinguish important material from trivial
- listening to an unenthusiastic, poorly organized, or monotone, or uncaring teacher.

11. Use *criterion-referenced* measurement and evaluation. This means that grades are based on what students can or cannot *do*, rather than where they rank in the class. Ranking students is termed *norm-referenced evaluation*; older students often call it "grading on the curve." It is more honestly called "grading on ability," and it typically results in a few persistent winners and a group of students with an academic life sentence of losing. In short, less capable students are forced into unfair competition, because no matter how much improvement they show, they still fall toward the bottom ranks. If a school system cherishes norm-referenced evaluation, teachers can at least try to mix in some criterion-referenced grading. Robert Slavin (1986, pp. 376-378) offers the above practical example of stirring criterion-referenced measurement into a traditional classroom recipe.

So extra points are given for personal progress. These extra points get added to the actual quiz score. Every couple of weeks, recalculate a new base line. Slavin also suggests adding more ingredients to assure that the recipe works: written praise, according to the number of improvement points, and communicating with parents about what you are doing and why.

Self-efficacy is related to arousal theory, which we discussed earlier in this chapter. Teachers who feel efficacious believe in their ability to produce optimum arousal, and they probably are more effective in doing so. Students who feel efficacious are automatically more alert, because they expect success, are motivated to work toward it, and tend to enjoy the tasks that bring success.

In summary, it is a good thing to have self-efficacy and to encourage its development in learners. A student with strong efficacy beliefs is motivated—not discouraged—by gaps between goals and performance. Best of all, self-efficacy is not an enduring personality trait. It is manipulable, and it responds to changes in the classroom environment. That makes teachers more important than ever!

Attributions For Success and Failure

There are other self-beliefs that influence motivation and accomplishment in the classroom. Bernard Weiner (1979) and his colleagues have developed a theory that considers causes *and* consequences of classroom behavior. His ideas reflect what social psychologists call *attribution theory*, for reasons the following examples should make clear:

- Danny got a C- on a test. He attributes his mediocre grade to the test's being too tough.
- Fred also got a C-. But he had not studied much in the week before the test, and figures he was lucky to get even what he did.
- Randy received an A. His ability earned it, he feels.
- Brian also got an A. He credits extra study for several days before the test.

The boys' differing attributions for their test performance are not just useful explanations of past behavior; they help to establish expectations for future behavior. Weiner has devised a scheme for classifying attributions that uses each of the four boys' explanations. The classification focuses, as Figure 4.2 shows, on two dimensions: *locus of control* and *stability*.

"Interesting," you may be saying to yourself, "but what will I do with that in the classroom?" Adding the dimension of stability provides important clues to what turns students on and off in school and what teachers can do to help turn them on and off, and that is what motivation is about. Stable characteristics such as ability are enduring, as their name implies, and difficult to change; unstable characteristics such as effort can be readily increased or decreased. The difficulty of a task—test, recitation, homework—is relatively stable but impersonal; someone else determines it. And luck, of course, is perceived to be unpredictable.

Attribution in the Classroom

All these aspects of attribution—ability, effort, task difficulty, and luck—are *perceived*, it is important to remember, not necessarily objectively real. Danny perceived the test as too hard, but Randy perceived it as fair enough. The subjectivity of perception helps to explain why students behave so differently under the same conditions, that is, why their motivation and performance varies when their environment does not. For example, students show more persistence at a task when they ascribe success to their own efforts. And their attributions also influence their preferences among tasks: Students seek tasks that accord with their usual attributions. If students judge that ability achieved their past successes, they will favor tasks that require competence rather than luck or special effort.

The attribution process occurs with our perceptions of others' behavior as well as our own, and teachers' perceptions of students probably influence much of what goes on in the classroom. In a series of studies summarized by Weiner (1972), teachers were provided data about some imaginary pupils—how the students ranked in ability, how hard each tried on a test, why each achieved on the test. Then this question was asked: How much reward or punishment did the students merit? The outcomes:

1. Regardless of their exam performance, students who were believed to have tried harder were better rewarded than those who appeared not to have tried.

2. Regardless of effort, students of little ability were rewarded more generously than those of high ability.

Figure 4.2   The Attribution Framework

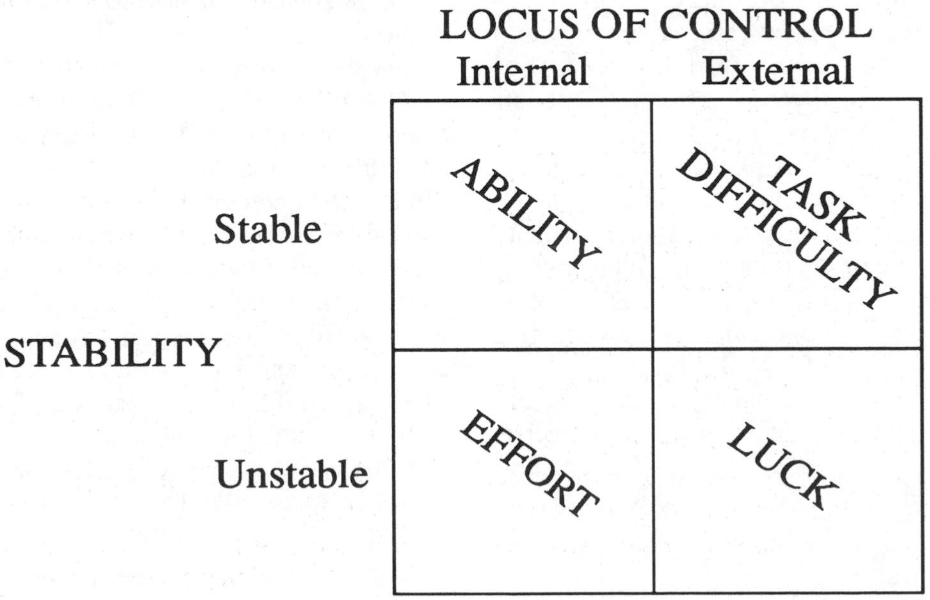

Add up the two outcomes and you will find that students of little ability and high effort got the best deal. Teachers seem to value effort above ability, especially if the student has surmounted the obstacle of low ability by strong effort. On the other hand, when failing students seem not to try, teachers hand out abundant criticism. If teacher attributions of students' performance lead to different consequences for different students, then teachers influence students even more than has been taken for granted.

Teachers cannot do anything *directly* about ability, because it is a durable characteristic. But they can alter self-beliefs about ability. Schunk (1985) demonstrated that self-efficacy and skill is enhanced when teachers deliver ability feedback (such as, "You're good at this!") as students progress. Teachers can also try to ensure that students understand that they can control the internal, unstable component of *effort*. Simple enough? No. It is more complex than it sounds, because internal and external factors interact to produce students' beliefs about success and failure. For example, difficult tasks, set up by the teacher and therefore externally controlled, require ability *and* effort for the student to succeed. With simple tasks it is possible to succeed on the basis of *either* ability or effort.

Here is another example of the complexity of internal and external attribution factors. Learning-disabled students sometimes think that effort is not very important as a cause of school success or failure (Licht, 1984). What would convince them that increased effort can make success more likely? Schunk and Cox (1986) showed that learning disabled students profit from effort feedback. (For example, "You've been working hard.") That sort of comment will improve their self-efficacy and performance, because it helps them to understand the importance of effort. On the other hand, the same sort of feedback with non-disabled students may be ineffective or even backfire. Weiner *et al.* (1983) point out that when students see a task as easy, praise coupled with effort feedback is interpreted as a suggestion of low ability.

This interaction of internal and external factors has direct implications for teaching. The teacher should set tasks that are *moderately* difficult, so that some ability and some effort will be required, but

because ability varies considerably among students, teachers should individualize tasks as much as possible. Any task assigned to all students, you can be fairly certain, may be meaningful and interesting to some and dreadful to others. This range of student interest will produce a mix of successes and failures. And as failures occur and continue, you will encounter student misbehavior: Misbehavior is the students' alternative means of motivation.

One problem in dealing with students who are prone to failure is that they may not react in the way that reinforcement theory predicts; if they are rewarded for effort they ought to try harder in the future. But Covington and Omelich (1977) have observed that some students do not respond to praise with increased effort and others actually reduce effort. Why? Because they have become inured to failure and expect it. Covington and Omelich hypothesize that when students have low efficacy beliefs about a particular task, they turn to protecting their self-esteem. To that end they pose as capable-but-not-trying, which is the opposite of what impresses teachers, trying-but-not-capable. The pose would be destroyed, of course, by increased effort after reinforcement. Even more obviously, they take refuge in excuses. When such a student flunks a test, he does not quietly accept the mark: He explains with a straight face that he had not been able to study because his dog chewed up his notes, his reference books had been stolen, and the electricity in the house had been off for two days. GLD students are familiar with this ploy. In the past, their effort has frequently predicted failure. To protect a fragile sense of ability, they refuse to expend extra effort.

Can failure and unhealthy attributions be reduced? Covington and Omelich think so. They assert that the structure of most classrooms in which students compete with each other for grades, promotes excessive failure. They would change competition among students to self-competition, shift to mastery learning, or shift to cooperative learning teams where no one need fail. Also, transforming large assignments into a series of more manageable subgoals should promote success. Finally, contracting with students, which explicitly details student tasks, can give youngsters a less defensive sense of responsibility for schoolwork.

Shyness in the Attribution Pattern

In her study of GLD children, Baum (1985) coupled an attribution measure with an academic self-efficacy instrument. The child was asked how skilled he or she felt (self-efficacy) in various academic behaviors, such as doing a science project or taking important tests. Then for each behavior a child reported *ineptness*, a second question was asked: Why aren't you very good at this? The students' options were the usual attribution reasons—not smart (ability), don't try (effort), unlucky, or too hard (task difficulty). On a hunch, Baum included a fifth possible explanation: too shy. The data spoke loudly. Baum discovered that GLD children used "too shy" as an explanation for failure 26% of the time. Their LD peers offered the same attribution 14% of the time, and their gifted classmates only 3%. In other words, this single attribution clearly distinguished these three groups of students. Shyness, like ability, is viewed as an internal, stable attribute. When a student persists in explaining failure because of shyness (or lack of ability), it may lead to a sense of helplessness, and in turn, to avoidance of the very school tasks that need more practice.

Why should GLD youngsters blame shyness for their sense of school failure? There seem to be two reasons: one dealing with the environment, the other with genes. To preserve feelings of intelligence, GLD students may explain their failures by shyness. This sort of explanation can be a bluff in order to appear smart (or not dumb): "I could do it if I weren't so shy…" We have seen shyness—the behavior or interest in it—in a variety of situations. For example, a group of GLD fifth graders were producing a video documentary on embarrassment. They titled their production, "Where Are Earthquakes When We Need Them?" On other occasions, we have noted that some of these students seem afraid to interrupt the teacher to ask an important question or to relay information.

Like arousal, shyness is known to be influenced by heredity. Some children are born excessively timid. Ten to fifteen percent of us may enter life with a predisposition toward shyness. At the other extreme, some infants seem to leap audaciously into the world. But these biological differences do not automatically result in behavioral patterns that endure for life. They set the stage for the environment to operate, and environmental influences can modify temperamental style. Jerome Kagan (cited in Asher, 1987) remarks, "It takes more than simply a biological vulnerability to produce a [shy] child. You need a stressor plus the vulnerability" (p. 64).

Whatever the reasons for shyness, social hesitancy has strong influence on behavior and on others' impressions. Students need to feel secure enough to ask for clarification when they are confused about an idea or about directions. GLD students especially must be able to act as their own advocate and be assertive at the appropriate times.

The GLD child has a wild pattern of strengths and weaknesses that resembles nothing so much as Pinocchio's profile. It is a confusing and sometimes maddening combination, for the child as well as for parents and teachers. We speculate that the profile itself is an unusual and enduring stressor that may trigger shyness in the GLD child. The teacher's role, indirectly, is to reduce the impact of such a stressor. As we have said, boosting successes—especially by reinforcing the student's strengths—will help to develop coping skills and lessen timidity. Over the long run, tilting the balance of school experiences toward success will mean that there will be fewer failures for the student to explain.

No matter what motivational device is used, the reduction of failure should help to establish realistic and productive attributions. Remember, when students finish school, self-beliefs such as attributions and self-efficacy become tools for coping with the rest of life.

CHAPTER 5

COGNITION AND SELF-REGULATION

In Psychology, cognition encompasses the processes of thinking and learning: that is, how we acquire, store, and use information. At the highest level, it involves awareness and personal control of various strategies to learn and to perform. We will consider several theoretical and well-researched points about memory and self-regulation of learning, and then apply these points to gifted and learning-disabled students.

Although the philosophy of behaviorism has dominated psychology for much of this century, it has fallen short in explaining thought and memory. So interest in cognitive psychology has surged in recent years. Since thinking and knowing continue to be unobservable and difficult to measure, cognitive research must make inferences about mental processes by proposing models of mental behavior and then judging how well external evidence fits the models. The most usual cognitive model is termed *information processing*. The programming of computers has shaped this recent offshoot of cognitive psychology. Just as the computer manipulates sets of data, the brain transforms information to solve problems. The brain, of course, does more. It is already active and does not need an operator to turn on or to instruct it. It fashions new, original ways of processing information. Its plans are not so rigid as the programs; it is flexible and insightful. And it makes errors.

In the information processing view, human beings seek information, interpret it, organize, transform, and file it in memory. They also merge the information with other data already stored in their heads and act on the basis of it. The centerpiece of all this processing is memory.

Without memory, we could not learn. We could not even qualify as intelligent animals. Each time we reached into a tree to pluck a banana, we would have to discover anew that we had to peel the fruit before we could munch it. Each time we roved the shore in search of dinner, we would find out that oysters are edible and rocks are not. So, in effect, we are largely what we remember.

The capacity of the memory is awesome. Ordinary folk, in a lifetime, store billions of items of information in their memories, including some 50,000 words and a greater number of images—of scenes, objects, and faces Extraordinary folk may perform even more impressive feats of memory, at least in special ways. Leonardo da Vinci needed to see someone only once to draw a perfect likeness. The conductor Arturo Toscanini could set down accurately the score of a symphony he had not heard in forty years. A one-time Russian newspaper reporter known to psychologists only as "S" indicated that the *potential* of memory might be virtually boundless. Given a list of seventy unrelated objects, S could repeat it flawlessly, top to bottom or bottom to top, years later. S quit journalism for the stage, where in three shows a night he invited audiences to pepper him with nonsense syllables After the audience ran out of nonsense, S would write every syllable on a chalkboard. The chalkboard was soon scrubbed, but S's memory was not. Many performances later, he could still come up with the lists of syllables of any earlier night. S ascribed much of his curious ability to the phenomenon that he "tasted" and "saw" oral sounds and musical tones. Every voice, for him, had its distinctive color. A musical tone of a certain pitch and loudness felt, he said, like borsch on his tongue and appeared like a brown strip edged with red tongues in his mind. (Luria, 1968).

Memory—even with someone as unusual as S—seems to have three distinctive storage systems: sensory, short-term, and long-term. Although it is convenient to think of these systems as separate, it is more likely that they are related levels of a single, coherent memory structure.

Sensory Storage

Information in the form of environmental stimuli bombards us in great quantity and enters the sensory storage system. Evidence suggests that sensory storage holds accurate images of incoming stimuli while the brain searches for recognizable features or patterns. When familiarity is established—all this takes less than a couple of seconds—information is passed to short term storage. The irrelevant information decays immediately, and the sensory storage busily attends to new stimuli.

Can sensory storage attend to all incoming stimuli? Probably not, even in a quiet environment. There must be some filtering mechanism that sifts through the information. Several filter hypotheses have been advanced. Although there is little agreement, the most usual approach is called an *attenuated filter* (Triesman, 1964). This is a filter with a threshold that may be set high or low, depending on the intensity of the stimulus bombardment. In the ordinary setting, the filter lets only some of the stimuli through for examination and feature analysis. Certain important stimuli, such as your name spoken, will leap over the threshold and demand immediate and conscious attention. Other stimuli are let in the perceptual door but are not awarded such high status. They may sneak through consciousness and into behavior without any attention…unless you happen to think about what you are thinking or doing! Awareness and intentional control of memory's behavior is the foundation of *self-regulated learning*, about which we will say more shortly.

Short-Term Storage

Where does awareness of thinking or behavior take place? In short-term storage. Because con-

sciousness, or awareness, seems to occur here, some psychologists call short-term storage *working memory*, as if to underline its importance. The high status of short-term storage is something of an irony, because it has a puny capacity.

First, it holds information just long enough to sort it out and determine whether or not it merits keeping. If you remembered everything that happened to you, including every inane conversation along with the significant ones, your head would soon be cluttered with trivia. In short-term storage, we dismiss the trivia and pass on the worthwhile data to long-term storage. Sorting the trivia from the significant is an important function of short-term storage. It does this by *encoding*, or interpreting the images of stimuli sent from the sensory register. If you were asked what you have just read, you could not reproduce each word; that image has already decayed. But you could give the general meaning of the words, thanks to the encoding process. In general, short-term storage has only twenty or thirty seconds to sort and encode. After that time, information is either passed to long-term storage or lost from the system. Of course you can extend the short interval by re-entering the information: by reading, looking at, or hearing the information again. You can even re-hear it silently by thinking of it.

That does not mean you can stretch the usual thirty-second time limit into ten minutes. There will be other information bumping the thoughts out because of the second type of limited capacity in short term storage: There simply is not much room. In a classic article entitled "The Magical Number Seven, Plus or Minus Two," George Miller (1956) argued that we have space for five to nine bits of unrelated information at a time or, on average, seven. Many demonstrations have borne out Miller's contention. Today we know that the capacity of short-term storage develops with age. At age two, it can handle two bits of information, increasing gradually to its tiny maximum of about seven bits by age fifteen.

As we can extend the thirty second focus of short-term memory by re-entering information, we can also pack in more information by grouping or chunking it. Thus you should be able to dial a ten-digit phone number without looking back and forth in the book if the digits are chunked in a handy way. For example, the toll-free number 800-333-

5555 is probably treated as three bits of data, leaving enough short-term capacity to recall who and why you are calling. The apparent limitations of space and time in short-term storage also require that when you are introduced to someone you process the name into long-term storage right off. Short-term storage will not have the room to keep it for you, because incoming stimuli will boot it out of the way.

Long-Term Storage

On the other hand, the capacity of long-term memory, as we remarked earlier, is awesome. Yet most of us tend to think of it as rather limited and believe that if we do not use fairly often what we have learned, we forget it and lose it forever. Many studies have shown those folk wisdoms to be faulty. Some evidence for the durability of long-term memory comes from hypnosis, under which people recall events that elude them under normal conditions. Early evidence also came from electrical stimulation of the brain. In the 1940's Canadian neurosurgeon Wilder Penfield tried to locate in the brain the sites of epileptic seizures. Prodding with an electrode in a memory area, he found that patients, still awake, remembered long-faded occurrences. Moving the electrode released memories of different occasions. Despite this discovery, the physical structure of long-term storage remains a mystery, although speculation increases that brain chemicals interact with changes in connections among neurons.

The psychological structure—what activates long-term memory, how images are coded and stored, and how information is retrieved—is also unknown. Various researchers have proposed many coding systems. One of the simplest and most widely used is the two-part system suggested by John Anderson (1990). In Anderson's view, information may be coded as declarative knowledge (knowing **what**) or procedural knowledge (knowing **how**). Obviously these systems communicate with each other, because a procedural skill typically involves knowledge of height, weight, location, name, purpose, or other declarative information. For example, the student who knows how to store data on a computer's hard disk probably also can name the various parts of the keyboard (and will be most pleased to tell you).

No storage theory can explain how information or images are converted to biochemical matter, then reformed into thought or behavior. That difficulty has not slowed memory researchers. If the molecular route is too bewildering for now, then what can be learned from the larger picture of routine behavior? "Plenty!" they chorus. One of the most important big-picture discoveries is that long-term memory is not a passive storage device. It is active—although beneath our awareness—as it merges, creates, and modifies information. This constructive view of memory presents something of a paradox. On one side, it is an astonishing strength: It allows the formation of useful knowledge from the inside, and the creation of new ideas by merging others. It also permits, somehow, the comprehension of novel arrangements of information, such as a sentence that you have never read before.

On the dark side, the activity of long-term storage allows it to blend data into faulty or downright stupid information. As an example of long-term memory's constructive activity, Loftus and Palmer (1974) showed adults a film of an auto accident, then gave them questionnaires about it. But the questionnaire differed slightly. Half the subjects were asked, "About how fast were the cars going when they *smashed into* each other?" The other half were asked, "About how fast were the cars going when they *hit* each other?" (The italics are ours.) A week later, all subjects were asked, "Did you see any broken glass?" Of the subjects whose first question had used the word *smashed*, 32% said they had seen shattered glass; only 14% of the other group claimed to have seen broken glass. NO glass had been broken in the mishap. And the subjects who had been given the *smashed* question estimated the cars' speed at 30% greater than did those who had the *hit* question. This sort of creative but unintended restructuring has led some researchers to question the accuracy of eyewitness testimony in criminal trials (Loftus, 1979).

In short, evidence indicates that we pull together information from several sources to construct a "memory" of an event, and may employ, in retrieving from memory, information beyond our actual experiences. Long-term memory is a process that is highly active: We reorganize ideas and facts as we gain information, even if the information is incompatible with our experience.

Memory and Exceptional Students

Presumably, a child with a specific learning disability can have trouble in any of the three sequences of memory, from the sensory register to long-term storage. Difficulty in sensory storage, for example, might result from inadequate filtering of stimuli, so that the youngster attends to irrelevant information while ignoring the important. In short-term storage, the child may have trouble retaining or coding short sequences of information long enough to stash them into a more permanent location. When a faulty filter shovels meaningless data into short-term memory, the child may be bewildered trying to coax the information into long-term memory. Two external conditions increase the child's frustration. First, the teacher and parents usually convey an unmistakable expectation that lesson content should be learned. Second, when other students appear to be catching on, social comparisons speak loudly to the child struggling to merge material with memory.

Problems of long-term memory might involve overactive combining of information into incorrect beliefs, weak connections among related bits of information, difficulty retrieving information, or lack of self-regulation and awareness of learning behaviors. As we have said, the portions of memory are not isolated. Trouble with one memory process can impair other processes.

By contrast, the gifted child may have sharper attentional and filtering capacity in sensory storage, strong coding skills in short-term memory, and much more efficient access routes to information stored in long-term memory. Most notably, gifted individuals have large storehouses of information squirreled away in long-term memory. The material seems to be placed along a well-constructed scaffolding, so that there are clear routes from certain information to other information. The gifted person with creative talent also seems capable of rapidly erecting new scaffolding, especially along unpredictable routes.

What about the youngster who is both gifted and learning disabled? As usual, they are complex and little is known about whether their memory processes might be different. We can speculate, though, from personal observation and self-reports from such students. On the surface, they appear to have trouble with the stimulus filter in sensory storage and with the contents—the flow of consciousness—of short-term memory. They frequently seem inattentive to important points in a lesson: When the teacher is discussing proteins in the DNA molecule, Jonathan in considering whether he can build the molecule in origami style. When Jonathan actually starts fiddling around with a page torn from his notebook, his inattention becomes conspicuous. To the teacher, Jonathan is locked in a cycle: the less he pays attention, the poorer the learning, and the poorer the learning... However, one might ask whether Jonathan is doing anything useful with his memory when he appears inattentive. The answer is that he might be, but the material being coded and rehearsed diverges from the lesson plans. The challenge for the teacher is to motivate Jonathan to approach rather than to avoid the fare of the classroom.

GLD students are frequently quite interested in classroom topics, but their mental drumbeats get them marching out of step with the lesson. The child may be following a jazzy improvisational line, skimming here and dwelling there. Meanwhile, the teacher bangs out a methodical, even beat. A discussion about the Wright brothers' first manned flight in Kitty Hawk may set off imagery about strapping a jet propulsion engine onto the original rickety craft. Or it may stimulate a mental spin into a different area of scaffolding in long-term memory; this often results in private analogies. For example, the child might wonder why flying animals do not use propellers or jet engines, or why planes must. If the student makes the analogy public, an unprepared teacher may have difficulty fitting the analogy to the lesson plan.

As for the GLD student's long-term memory, the variety of information stored here is about as jagged as Pinocchio's profile. For content or skill areas of interest to the child, there is a sustained commitment—almost devotion—to the topic. During the period of commitment, a remarkable assortment of study behaviors step forward. The child will seek more information about the topic, from both people and written work. He or she will set about organizing the content in a way that is personally meaningful. And frequently the student will initiate some way of transforming the learning into a performance or product. This collection of behaviors is exactly the sort of outcome we expect of schooling—self-regulated learning (Zimmerman,

1989). The end result of all this effort is a substantial bank of information in long-term memory. Unfortunately, the accumulation may occur at the expense of other school topics, which means that long-term memory for those topics may be shallow and perhaps disconnected to other information on the mental scaffolding.

All humans, as we remarked in the Motivation chapter, seek arousing stimulation from their environment. Unless they have been taught to be helpless, they are curious and hungry to learn. To the extent the academic fare is made attractive, children will gobble it. But like foods, careful selection and balance of choices is essential. The student with deficiencies in specific knowledge or behavior needs academic supplements; the youngsters obsessed with a topic needs encouragement to consider a more well-rounded academic diet. In one sense, both types of imbalance are characterized by underperformance. By definition, academic deficit involves poor learning or performance. Academic excesses create deficits indirectly, because they limit opportunity for other types of learning. It is useful to remember that the GLD student is usually quite successful in areas or skills that are personally important. That simple observation implies that the student has a repertoire of learning strategies that have been used. However, the GLD student may need reminders, and possibly demonstrations, that learning strategies can be useful in other situations. After enough practice, the student should become proficient enough at strategy generalization that no external reminders are needed. The student's learning is now self-regulated. In the next chapter, we detail two case studies that show how strategies may be generalized to make new learning more interesting to the GLD student.

Memory and Self-Regulated Learning

We have remarked about the irony of short-term storage: Although its capacity is tiny, it is the workhorse of memory. It is here that a person can reflect, evaluate, and plan. Of course, there is constant interaction with long-term storage; short-term memory continually retrieves information to be used in solving problems. Once solved, a problem's solution—and perhaps the procedure—may be translated into immediate performance or filed away

for later reference.

In school, the typical problems involve academic learning, that is, how to store knowledge and skills in long-term memory, and then retrieve them at will. Competent learners acquire strategies for saving information in their mental banks. Those strategies pay substantial dividends when they prompt ideas about combining or revising strategies to make learning more efficient. But knowledge and use of strategies, at least initially, depends on awareness. The student must put the strategy in mental view, in short-term memory, and she must predict whether the strategy will work with a particular problem, or if the strategy needs revision. While a problem is tackled, the student must evaluate whether the strategy is helping to make progress. This collection of strategy knowledge, selection, and use is termed *self-regulated learning*.

Academic self-regulation involves three broad activities (Borowski, *et al.*, 1987). First, a student must learn a variety of specific strategies for learning content and skills, for example, taking a history test that requires comparison of different concepts or forming a reasonable estimate about a long-division solution. But it is more than the mechanical use of memorized strategies. Self-regulation means that the learner can make decisions about when and whether to apply the strategy, and once engaged, can monitor the strategy's usefulness.

Second, the student must be able to use the strategies in various situations and environments. That is, he must generalize and adapt the problem-solving skill to new areas. For example, having learned how to distinguish apparently similar ideas in geography, she might find that strategy useful in an English class. And third, the child needs a sense of capability—self-efficacy—in applying the strategies. The first two areas involve knowledge and skill; the third, self-efficacy, deals with motivation. It is self-efficacy that helps to transform the knowledge into action. Without a feeling of capability, strategy knowledge may be acquired, but it is likely to remain inert until the student believes the strategy can result in some successful behavior. When a student is convinced that effort at using a strategy will produce success, he is likely to construct a "cognitive simulation" of a learning activity (Bandura, 1989). Apart from the task itself, the learner will visualize himself using a strategy successfully. That mental rehearsal will help to apply the strategy when an actual problem appears. The more the strategy is practiced, in simulation and with actual tasks, the more the student will believe that strategy use is under personal control. Coupled with outcomes that seem beneficial, a sense of personal control is a powerful steering wheel in school learning. In summary, academic self-regulated learning is built on three requirements. That is a tall order for any student, especially when teachers expect students to pay attention to external advice. External advice *is* required, initially, to help implant self-regulation. But teachers—and parents—frequently forget that the eventual goal is academic self-regulation. The more prompting, cajoling, persuading, and assisting provided by the external environment, the less the student will practice internal direction. The external steering must fade away while the child becomes more competent at driving his own learning.

The fact that there are these three requirements of self-regulated learning means that it is hard to succeed. Failure can occur when any of the three parts is deficient. This also makes the teacher's job more difficult, because it requires a keen diagnostic sense about which area is faulty, plus skill at boosting the weak area. Teachers of learning-disabled youngsters must be especially patient. Although LD students can be deficient in any (or all) of the three areas, those children are frequently weakest in the second and third areas—transferring a strategy to a new situation and self-efficacy about

using effective strategies. Even when the task is highly similar to one in which the strategy has been applied, the LD child often has difficulty understanding that the strategy can be reapplied (Douglass, 1981; Gelzheiser, 1984).

Strategy generalization is essential in reading, partly because most narrative passages are somewhat novel. Also, reading itself is an underlying skill that serves the learning of other content. For the skillful learner, reading becomes automatic after a time, and the brain can concentrate on the content of the printed material. For the child with feeble reading strategies, the fob has now doubled in size: The struggle of reading combined with uncertainty about new information will almost certainly overload short-term memory. The problem takes a different angle for certain students who have trouble monitoring comprehension during reading. The child may plod through page after page and be utterly baffled when, at the end of the assignment, nothing has been stored in long-term memory.

Awareness and personal control of learning, the core of self-regulation, become vastly easier if a student desires the outcomes of learning and believes the learning is useful. It is a stiff challenge to the teacher to convert the entire curriculum into something tasty, especially when twenty-two classroom customers have different tastes! In the next chapter, we consider two case studies of GLD children, and illustrate how their teachers encouraged them to use self-regulated behaviors.

CHAPTER 6

RECOGNITION AND APPLICATION OF INTELLECTUAL STRENGTHS

In the first section of this book, we detailed case studies of children whose talent is of a special sort—children who can realize their potential only through activities that focus the talent. The general characteristics of these children also were described and the opaque terminology sometimes applied to these children has, we hope, become a little clearer.

Throughout this discussion we revisited one central question: How is it possible for a child to be both exceptionally talented and disabled at the same time? We explored this question by describing seemingly contradictory behaviors a teacher and parent might see in a child. Earlier in this section we delved further into the question of "why?" by offering certain theories of motivation and learning useful in explaining the cognitive underpinnings of inconsistent behaviors exhibited by GLD students.

Another useful way for us to understand the GLD phenomenon is to re-examine the information gleaned from the student's performance on the WISC-R. Although school psychologists and learning disabilities specialists rely heavily on WISC-R patterns to diagnose the problem and to specify an appropriate educational program, they usually do not consider the meanings that can be derived from the unique patterns suggested in Chapter 3. Most often the scores are used to confirm that there is a disability and in what areas the student is having difficulty. Moreover, discrepancies between verbal and performance IQ dominate decisions made on the student's behalf. But subtest patterns are rarely used to identify giftedness or to provide an environment that allows the gift to emerge and develop. Our objective in this chapter is to show how patterns of scores help to explain

why the child demonstrates wild shifts in learning behaviors. Then we will describe how these patterns can be used to enrich strengths and improve classroom learning behaviors of the GLD student.

Integrative Versus Dispersive Intelligence

As mentioned in Chapter 3, researchers have found that GLD students are generally strong in abstract holistic tasks and much weaker in tasks involving sequencing and memorizing isolated facts. Two of the studies described based their analysis of Bannatyne's (1974) recategorization model. This approach has given us insight into interpreting the learning behaviors of GLD students, but it falls short on implications for better serving this special population. A more comprehensive, flexible model is suggested by John Dixon (1989) in his work with WISC-R patterns with GLD students. He has theorized that these students have particular strengths in what he terms *Integrative Intelligence*. They also demonstrate severe weaknesses in *Dispersive Intelligence*. This discrepancy explains why GLD students can be brilliant in creative endeavors while simultaneously failing the weekly spelling test. The next sections will describe Integrative and Dispersive Intelligence and provide examples of how different aspects of school require differing abilities in the two types of thinking.

Integrative Intelligence is the capacity to understand and discover patterns and connections in broad expanses of information. This ability enables a learner to solve problems in otherwise unanticipated ways. Its importance lies in the fact that unusual creative accomplishments—whether of an artistic, scientific, or humanistic sort—require a deep level of integrated knowledge in the area of endeavor. This knowledge is so profound that pieces or elements of that knowledge can be changed, experimented with, manipulated, or viewed from an entirely different perspective without violating or losing a grasp of the essential principles, patterns, and connections in that area of knowledge.

This playing around within an integrated system of wisdom is almost always an essential ingredient in creative accomplishment, whether this involves composing a symphony, writing a novel, creating a new mathematical formulation, or discovering a new twist in the nature of matter. Integrative Intelligence is essentially what Konrad Lorenz meant when he talked about "gestalt" conception. "The scientist, confronted with a multitude of irregular and apparently irreconcilable facts, suddenly 'sees' the general regularity ruling them all" (Lorenz, 1951, cited in Dixon, 1983, p.136).

It is not uncommon to find descriptions of this kind of thinking given by some to the great geniuses of history when they are asked to account for their own uniqueness. Einstein described his thought process thus:

> The psychological entities which seem to serve as elements in thought are certain signs and more or less clear images which can be voluntarily reproduced and combined.... It is also clear that the desire to arrive finally at logically connected concepts is the emotional basis of this rather vague play.... This combinatory play seems to be the essential feature in productive thought (Dixon, 1983. p.93).

In a partly biographical accounting of intelligence, the mathematician Doug Hofstadter interpreted encounters with thinking similarly:

> As I have gotten older, I have come to see that there are inner mental patterns underlying our ability to conceive of mathematical ideas. Universal patterns in human minds that make them receptive not only to the patterns of mathematics but also to abstract regularities of all sorts in the world.... Indeed, how could anyone hope to approach the concept of beauty without deeply studying the nature of formal patterns and their organizations and relationships to mind? (Hofstadter, 1985, p.177).

Is this kind of thinking required during the school day? If so, which tasks require students to understand patterns and see the bigger picture? Creative writing, grasping the underlying idea of a story, drawing conclusions, understanding when to add, subtract, multiply or divide all require integrative thinking. Other examples include designing and conducting a scientific experiment, building a model of the Titanic for a social studies project, or drawing a mural of Indian life. In short, these activities all require a sense of the whole and how the pieces come together to form a meaningful pattern. Students must supply relevant details as they work to complete their envisioned plan. As we have noted, both gifted students and GLD students appear to have little difficulty with tasks requiring this type of thinking.

Dispersive Intelligence, on the other hand, complements Integrative Intelligence. It allows us to remember and use isolated facts and associations that need not make sense in any big context, such as the name of a faded actress who slapped a policeman in Hollywood or your phone number. It needs to be understood that, in the routine of daily living, Dispersive Intelligence is of equal importance with Integrative Intelligence. For example, it is very important to be able to associate the spoken word "enough" with the letter sequence e-n-o-u-g-h rather than with the sequence e-n-u-f. From the point of view of the phonetic pattern consistency (that is, Integrative Intelligence), the second letter sequence seems more reasonable than the first. The strength of Dispersive Intelligence is that it allows limited association between a certain vocalized sound pattern, "enough," and a certain letter sequence to be accepted for what it is. This is done without interference from the broader attempts at patterned understanding (phonetic consistency) which might suggest it should be otherwise.

Another example can be given from arithmetic. It is handy for a person to remember that "9x7=63" without having to discover or figure out that fact through some sort of reference to number patterning. This is a little different from the spelling problem given above in that one could arrive at a math fact by some process of pattern reconstruction such as "3x7=21", "3x3=9", therefore, "9x7=3x21=63." There are some children who use Integrative Thinking of this sort to reconstruct math facts, but it is a very clumsy way to deal with math facts.

The extent that a student possesses strong Dispersive Intelligence and uses it influences school success. For this child, it is perfectly acceptable to recall that "enough" is spelled e-n-o-u-g-h. It will not help to construct a theory of spelling, a model of spelling, or a gestalt of spelling that would lead one to conclude that "enough" be spelled the way it is. This is the power of Dispersive Intelligence. It lightens the intellectual load when it is employed properly.

The distinction between Integrative and Dispersive Intelligence helps to explain why some children can be simultaneously capable and disabled. Dispersive Intelligence is the thing most extensively rewarded in most elementary schools. No matter what other amazing things a child might accomplish, if the child does not master the dispersive details of reading, writing, and arithmetic, all else is likely to appear insignificant compared to the failure in conventional knowledge. The learner might create an intricately interesting sculpture or produce a TV program. But, if unable to remember from day to day (or even minute to minute) the spelling of "enough" or that "9x7=63," the student is likely to be considered a failure. If unable to remember what was assigned for homework or where a math book was left, how can this student be considered bright, responsible, or even gifted?

To stretch this idea further, consider the paragraph and cartoon on the opposite page. A student was asked by his fifth-grade teacher to write an opinion of the 1991 war in the Middle East. The differences between the two products represent the dilemma GLD students face. With poor verbal mechanics they often cannot express their creative ideas in writing. Written work may call more attention to their disabilities than their abilities.

We have described students who appear to have strong abilities in Integrative Intelligence and much weaker in Dispersive Intelligence. Are they gifted or disabled? The answer is obviously both. The emphasis one places on the giftedness or the disability depends on the values brought to the judgement. If a person is interested in creative production that rests on integrative thinking, the disability will be set aside to consider the potential the student demonstrates for gifted behavior. On the other hand, if one is judging children primarily in terms of high academic achievement, the creativity might seem like an interesting but irrelevant sideshow. In the elementary school classroom, when such differences between Integrative Intelligence and Dispersive Intelligence occur, Dispersive Intelligence usually rules.

In making this assertion we do not imply that children have a good balance between the two, and there are some very bright youngsters who possess both in complementary abundance. However, some children are strong in integrative thinking and weak in tasks requiring Dispersive Intelligence. Consider these two children. Betty is strong in Integrative Intelligence and weak in Dispersive areas. George, on the other hand, has strength in Dispersive Intelligence but has difficulty in tasks requiring Integrative Intelligence.

In social studies, Betty cannot remember the name of a state capital or the date of a historical event, but she will suddenly become animated and sophisticated in talking about a trend in history or the implications of a social problem. George follows the opposite pattern. In science, George will memorize the new terminology with ease. Betty will not, but she will readily grasp theoretical links in scientific information. The pattern followed by most GLD students, as you may have surmised, is similar to that of Betty—high in Integrative Intelligence, but low in Dispersive.

Measuring Integrative Intelligence

We now need to consider how the distinction between Integrative and Dispersive Intelligence ties directly to the situation faced by many learning-disabled students. The connection is most apparent in diagnostic test score patterns. When diagnostic procedures are carried out for identifying a child as learning disabled, a number of tests can be used. The number and variety of those tests invite confusion, but there is one point of common ground that runs through much of this testing: the WISC-R. The WISC-R is administered to more learning-disabled students than any other instrument. This is justly so. The WISC-R subtests catch many of the subtle patterns that distinguish most learning-disabled children.

The interpretive value of the WISC-R is, unfortunately, often overlooked. Emphasis is usually placed on deriving either a full-scale IQ score or the Verbal and Performance IQs and the more

Creative Expression of a Fifth Grader

This short paragraph reflects little originality or abstract thought. The poor spelling, simplistic vocabulary, and poor handwriting scream out at the reader. In short, there seems to be no evidence of gifted potential shown by this piece of writing.

Hussein is a bad ruler. He is forsing Kuwayts out of there home. The U.S. and the Allies will try to stop him. Who will win

His LD resource room teacher, however, knowing that the student had much more to say about the war suggested that he draw a political cartoon instead. Here we find strong evidence of the student's metaphorical thinking when he represents Hussein as a dragon torching the Kuwaitees represented as the tiny victim. His grave concern about the allies' chance for victory was concisely expressed in his caption. (The original cartoon was done in color.)

meaningful subtest patterns are overlooked. When researchers conduct studies on the WISC-R, they never find that it divides neatly into a verbal section and a performance section (see Chapter 3). Although patterns underlying this test vary from study to study, these patterns are always more interesting than the verbal-performance split. The actual patterns found point consistently to the difference between Integrative and Dispersive Intelligence.

One way of organizing the WISC-R is on the basis of subtests in which learning-disabled students do well and those in which they do poorly. The Australian psychologist Colin MacLeod (1965) brought together information from eight different research studies in which this kind of comparison was made. The findings, summarized in Table 6.1, are surprisingly regular. LD children dependably show certain weaknesses and also certain strengths.

In a similar study of our own, we studied the WISC-R patterns of fifty fourth-, fifth- and sixth-grade students diagnosed as learning disabled in language arts (reading, writing, or spelling) and who spent their mornings in a resource room for language instruction. We were looking for learning-disabled children who had subtest scores high enough to suggest potential giftedness. The criterion for selection was a subtest score at the ninety-seventh percentile or higher. The results are listed in Table 6.2.

The pattern that emerges from such studies reveals that LD students can be quite talented on spatial tasks such as Block Design. They also can do very well on tasks that require recognition of patterned sequences such as Picture Arrangement. Abstract conceptualization can also be a strength, as shown on the Similarities subtest. On the other hand, they usually have problems on tests of detailed memory. This shows up on the Arithmetic subtest where the student's ability to apply math concepts is contingent upon instant recall of math facts. These students may also have trouble with meaningless sequencing as is required on the Digit Span subtest, and can be quite slow in the processing of details as measured by the Coding subtest.

A sophisticated statistical tool called factor analysis is sometimes used to study the dimensions running through the WISC-R. Although the results depend somewhat on the kinds of children studied, the usual pattern is summarized in Table 6.3. The WISC-R subtests are arranged in a sequence of

Table 6.1   MacLeod Studies of WISC Patterns

Subtest	Number of studies in which subtest was a strength for LD student	Number of studies in which subtest was a weakness for LD student
Block Design	5	0
Picture Arrangement	4	0
Comprehension	4	0
Picture Completion	3	0
Similarities	3	0
Object Assembly	2	0
Vocabulary	2	3
Digit Span	0	3
Information	0	6
Arithmetic	0	7
Coding	0	7

Table 6.2   Extreme Cognitive Strengths of LD Students

Subtest	*Percentage of LD students scoring in the 97th %tile or above*
Object Assembly	12%
Picture Arrangement	12%
Block Design	10%
Picture Completion	6%
Similarities	6%
Comprehension	6%
Information	6%
Vocabulary	4%
Digit Span	0%
Arithmetic	0%
Coding	0%

strongest to weakest performance.

The order of groupings in Table 6.3 is the most common strength-to-weakness pattern for learning-disabled students. The top three areas can often indicate distinct talent. The bottom three many times suggest the presence of a specific learning disability. This factor analysis distinction is consistent with the split between Integrative and Dispersive Intelligence. The top three groupings have their foundation in the capacity to discern broad patterns and connections in visual or verbal information. This is exactly what we mean by Integrative Intelligence. The bottom three areas have their foundation in accepting and remembering simple associations and meaningless sequences. Such descriptions define Dispersive Intelligence.

The contrast between Integrative Intelligence and Dispersive Intelligence makes much more sense than the traditional definitions of learning disabilities. For example, in legal terms, a learning disability is often defined as a gross discrepancy between intelligence and academic performance. When the child's school performance lags behind the level predicted by the IQ score, it is assumed that there must be some kind of specific disability. This traditional definition has virtually no meaning for un-

Table 6.3   Strength to Weakness Pattern for LD Students

Subtest Categories

Spatial Manipulation
    Block Design
    Object Assembly
Patterned Sequencing
    Picture Arrangement
    Mazes
Abstract Conceptualization
    Similarities
    Comprehension

Conventional Knowledge
    Vocabulary
    Information
Detailed Memory
    Arithmetic
    Picture Completion
Quick Detailed Processing
    Coding
Meaningless Sequencing
    Digit Span

derstanding the student's cognitive behavior.

Another popular definition is based on a discrepancy between the Verbal IQ and Performance IQ. Psychologists who use this definition can be looking for the imbalance to go in either direction (Verbal, high; Performance, low; or the opposite pattern). Unfortunately, the distinction is so general that it specifies little. It is another case of trying to get a sharp view of a specimen through a smudged lens. In the first place, it is often the case that low scores on the Verbal Scale are interpreted as a student's general inability to deal with verbal information. However, a low Verbal IQ does not preclude outstanding abilities on verbal comprehension tasks and other language-based activities that are part of a meaningful context, (a profile characteristic of many GLD students). Digit Span and Arithmetic subtest scores are usually responsible for a low Verbal IQ performance.

Lumping Performance subtests together creates a similar difficulty. If the child follows a fairly typical pattern, there will be an average or higher score on Spatial subtests with a somewhat lower score on Coding. When the two types of tasks are averaged together, information about the student is lost. Unfortunately, this situation is typical for GLD students, and documentation of specific abilities in complex cognitive activities is often overlooked.

From the very beginning of the learning disabilities movement, it was natural that the idea of discrepancy would have provided a way of thinking about these youngsters. Discrepancy is a metaphor for their lives. The important thing is for psychologists to continue refining the way discrepancies are defined. The discrepancy between IQ and school performance was a good start, and the discrepancy between Performance IQ and Verbal IQ was a step forward. Our position is that the discrepancy between Integrative Intelligence and Dispersive Intelligence moves us closer to a sensible diagnostic scheme.

Using the Information

In summary, gifted, learning-disabled students seem to have intellectual strengths in Integrative Intelligence that enable them to see underlying patterns and connections in broad concepts and abstract ideas. In contrast, they exhibit an inability to perform well in tasks involving Dispersive Intelligence such as remembering isolated facts and associations for which they see no wider connection. As was mentioned earlier in the chapter, this discrepancy helps to explain why GLD students have so much difficulty with relatively simple tasks while being able to complete more creative and complex assignments with relative ease.

In Table 6.3 we organized groupings of WISC-R subtests into particular cognitive skills and then divided them into Integrative Intelligence and Dispersive Intelligence. These patterns can give guidance for recognizing strengths of the GLD student and for creating more opportunities for school success. The first important use of these patterns is to assist us in determining whether particular LD students demonstrate the potential for gifted behavior. This potential can be easily documented by superior abilities in Integrative Intelligence. High scores on subtests included in Integrative Intelligence provide evidence that such students can think abstractly, see patterns, and make connections among ideas—all pieces of creative productivity.

A second implication of using pattern analysis is to use the information obtained from the patterns of strengths on subtests of the WISC-R to understand how the student learns best. This awareness along with knowledge of the student's interest are the essential ingredients needed to provide the student with the optimum environment for success. In such an environment, not only can the GLD student achieve something of personal pride and importance, but he can also begin to identify the strategies he used to accomplish his goal.

To understand how this process works, let us examine two case studies. Each of the students described below had been identified as learning disabled and had been nominated by their parents or teachers to participate in a state-funded program for GLD students. Our first task was to determine whether these students had high scores on Integrative Intelligence. Once that was confirmed, we then had to decide what particular abilities the youngster demonstrated and how these talents are applied to real life endeavors. In the following discussion, we describe how we used the WISC-R scores and other information to create an exciting curriculum where these students would be naturally motivated to achieve and apply cognitive strategies to relevant, challenging and complex tasks.

Louis

by Gail Herman

Louis, a sixth grader, had been identified as learning disabled because of his extreme difficulty in learning to read and write. His teachers also reported that he was easily distracted and a real "itch" in the classroom. For the past two years his parents and teachers had noticed a decline in his enjoyment of school and an increase in inappropriate behavior in the classroom. Table 6.4 shows Louis' WISC-R scores categorized into Integrative and Dispersive Intelligences.

Notice that Louis' performance in Integrative Intelligence is high. As we can see from Louis' test scores, he does extraordinarily well on tasks involving the understanding of social expectations (Comprehension), using and comprehending the spoken word (Vocabulary) and noticing details especially in a visual context (Picture Completion). These abilities are essential in writing, acting and social interactions of all sorts. Because he is capable in both what he sees (nonverbal) and hears (verbal), we might expect Louis to be competent in interpersonal skills as well. To gain some more information on the kinds of activities Louis preferred, we administered two learning style inventories: *Ways of Learning Scale* (Dixon, 1986) and *Myself and Others* (Dixon, 1986; See Appendix B). His responses indicated that he preferred self-initiated activities that involved verbal, social interaction and were creative. For example, his favorite school activities involved getting up and speaking in front of the class and doing group assignments. Louis also described how much he enjoyed writing stories, poems, and songs for his own enjoyment.

We have found that students such as Louis often think and learn and communicate much like actors. Such students use the larger context, visual and social, to comprehend and remember the details of a situation. They communicate best what they know through dramatic expression. In fact, they often create their own drama whenever possible. It should be no surprise that many GLD students find a home on the stage in their adult lives.

According to Gardner (1983), acting involves high skills in both kinesthetic and personal intelligence. This means that certain folks have the talent of reading people

Table 6.4   WISC-R Profile of Louis

Integrative Pattern		Dispersive Pattern	
Block Design	12	Arithmetic	10
Object Assembly	11	Digit Span	9
Picture Arrangement	11		
Mazes	—		
Similarities	13		
Comprehension	18		
Vocabulary	18		
Information	13		

and situations well. They are particularly sensitive to social and emotional dynamics in their environment such as moods, subtle meanings, and interpersonal relationships happening around them. In fact, these nonverbal messages oftentimes take priority over other verbal information simultaneously conveyed. These individuals respond to both motion and emotion to understand their world and to communicate what they know. Similar to actors, storytellers, and mimes, they are often able to incorporate other people's temperaments, motivations, and intentions into a spoken or dramatic presentation. T9hese abilities are crucial in a variety of real world endeavors. For instance, successful counselors, politicians, lawyers, social workers and teachers all have the ability to decode and encode verbal and nonverbal messages in a variety of social contexts.

When we find this pattern of strength in GLD students, three responsibilities step forward. The first is to help them to sharpen their abilities in verbal or dramatic expression. Next we need to assist these students in understanding the strategies they used in mastering tasks involved in this area. Third, we must teach these students to use these strategies in other tasks as well. Recall that these steps were described in Chapter 5 as encouraging self-regulated behavior.

Special enrichment programs purposefully designed to accentuate a particular talent have been successful in helping us to meet these responsibilities. In Louis' case, we established a ten-week program in dramatic expression in which students such as Louis could have an opportunity to use and perfect their dramatic ability for a real world purpose. (A complete description of this kind of program is given in Chapter 8). Following is an account of how Louis performed in the program. Notice how Louis was naturally motivated to engage in self-regulated behavior because the expected outcome was in an area of interest and strength for the students.

The Program (Louis)

At the first meeting of the program in dramatic expression, the mentor, a professional storyteller, explained to the students that they were chosen because they had a particular talent in drama. Louis became noticeably excited about the possibility of performing in the State Storytelling Festival to be held later that spring. The mentor encouraged him to work on one of his own stories to perfect it for the festival. During the program, the mentor assisted Louis in mastering the techniques of the professional storyteller so that he could perform with pride at the State Storytelling Festival. First, Louis needed to find a method of remembering his story other than by rote memorization so that his story could be told within a six-minute time frame and appear fresh each time he told it. Two methods which helped him were visual mapping and the incorporation of mimetic movements, facial expressions, and gestures with his characterizations. These techniques served as mnemonic devices. The visual map, a graphic depiction of the story's settings and important events, served as a picture in his mind's eye. The movements and gestures were kinesthetic cues which linked one emotional event with the next in the story. These helped Louis to keep the events of the story in mind as he retold his tale. He was now ready for performance techniques.

He practiced the beginning of his story while standing, sitting, and moving around freely to find the most comfortable delivery. He practiced using eye contact and looking at the top of people's heads to keep from being distracted. Because there would be a microphone at the Festival, he practiced with one. During feedback sessions, Louis sought constructive criticism. He tried some of the ideas, discarding some and keeping others. The results showed great variety of movement and voice. Louis was, in fact, a professional storyteller, focusing his attention on the effects his verbal and nonverbal behaviors would have on his audience.

Louis did attend the state Storytelling Festival and shared his story with students from many other schools. His devotion to his art form was evident from the amount of time and concentration he gave to it. His talent in storytelling was obvious from his stellar performance. This achievement greatly enhanced Louis' motivation and self-efficacy. He was willing to expend effort on learning his part. His ability to attend to the task at hand and take responsibility for his own success was evident. In addition, Louis used a variety of self-regulating behaviors en route to success. Let us take a moment to consider what skills were needed and how Louis accomplished them. Table 6.5 lists the personal adaptations of the self-regulation strategies used to complete the project.

Interestingly, the strategies involved in Louis' accomplishment were the very learning skills that GLD students cannot seem to apply in school. The next step then is to show students that, in fact, they are efficacious in using learning strategies and that they are capable of applying them to other learning situations.

Table 6.5   Louis' Application of Self-Regulation Strategies

Self-Regulation Strategies	*Personal Applications*
Memorizing sequence and details of the story	Using visual mapping to recall story details Using body movements as kinesthetic cues to link story events
Rehearsing and Overlearning	Having high self-set standards for performance at the story-telling festival, and practicing well beyond initial point of mastery
Focusing attention	Applying specific tips to avoid distractions, such as focusing on tops of heads while speaking
Using feedback during rehearsal	Gauging fit between ongoing speaking performance and goals. Locating rough spots in performance. Soliciting and listening to advice. Transforming advice into performance.

Mike

Mike, twelve-year-old LD student, had been placed in a self-contained classroom for LD students because of poor skills in writing, spelling and articulation. His reading was described as slow and labored but just this year his reading comprehension scores reached grade level. His teachers described Mike as "struggling with school work, worrying constantly and having little self-confidence." Table 6.6 summarizes Mike's WISC-R scores.

From these scores in Table 6.6 we can see that Mike is highly able in tasks requiring Integrative Intelligence. Unlike Louis, however, Mike's strongest areas are visual and spatial. His high Similarities score was probably due to his ability to see connections among things. For instance, consider this item found on the Similarities subtest, "How are a mountain and a lake alike?" A student strong in spatial concepts can readily conclude that both are geographical features as seen on a map. Mike's profile suggests that he is a spatial thinker, and information about his learning style preferences and interests corroborates this. His responses to items on the Ways of Learning Scale confirmed his strong interest in spatial mechanical ability. He consistently chose answers that showed a preference for visual information over verbal activities and a strong desire for choices. His hobbies included building models and sketching out ideas before solving a problem.

This pattern of exceptional abilities in spatial areas is prevalent in many GLD students. (Dixon, 1983; Silverman, 1989). These students typically score well on spatial manipulation and patterned sequencing subtests on the WISC-R. They spend time at home playing at such things as blocks, building models, clay sculptures, paper folding and creating other three-dimensional constructions. Puzzles and games that require actual manipulation such as Pick-Up Sticks, Tip It, and the Rubiks Cube can provide hours of amusement for these youngsters. Some prefer two-dimensional activities involving painting, drawing and other artistic activities. Architecture, engineering and careers in the visual arts are some real word applications of spatial abilities.

Table 6.6   Mike's WISC-R Profile

Integrative Pattern		*Dispersive Pattern*	
Block Design	14	Arithmetic	13
Object Assembly	18	Coding	9
Picture Arrangement	17	Digit Span	10
Mazes	13	Picture Completion	14
Similarities	15		
Comprehension	14		
Vocabulary	15		
Information	14		

Although these students may have differing interests and specific talents based on other areas of strengths, they share similarities in the way they think, organize information and communicate what they know. Dixon describes such individuals as having "the capacity to put the world together inside one's head such that all things relate to all others in precisely understood ways. The distance and directional positioning between a whole host of objects is so well understood that all become part of an interconnected system." (1983, p. 9) For example, it is this kind of ability that allows a person walking through a complex building to go from one location to another without becoming confused. It is as if people particularly strong in these abilities carry a three-dimensional map inside their head which is continually reoriented. These children usually have the ability to use visual rather than verbal methods to solve problems, generate ideas, organize information and communicate what they know. Many show an exceptional ability in mathematical reasoning and in appreciating the scope and significance of history. Because they think in images and can see a variety of patterns and interconnections among things, they tend to have rich imaginations. However, they may not be able to explain the steps by which they arrived at a conclusion because the solution may have suddenly appeared to them.

Spatial ability as described above, can be manifested in activities that are spatial mechanical or visual spatial. Mike showed definite preference for the former. He thoroughly enjoyed designing and actually building models. For example, in an activity designed to spot engineering talent, the students in Mike's class were asked to construct balloon-driven model cars. They were told that a prize would be given to the students whose car would go the farthest. Mike produced the best model. His attention to details such as how to reduce friction on the wheels, how to get more traction, and how to increase thrust proved that he had more technical knowledge and problem-solving skills than his peers did. His model won him a place in a specially designed program for the young engineer. The following description conveys how Mike was able to identify his own self-regulating strategies crucial to creating a high quality product.*

The Program (Mike)

At the onset of the program, the students were told that they would be required to build an original model of something interesting to them. Soon after the program began, Mike brought in an article that he had read about the efforts of engineers to build a rover vehicle for exploring Mars. The article described the problems such a project entailed, especially in regard to the unique landscape of the planet. Mike was so excited about this challenge that he decided to create his own prototype. It would have to include such features as remote control and a special arm built for manipulating objects. The instructor of the class was somewhat concerned about the complexity of the problem, but Mike would not be dissuaded. He argued that he had been studying the article and already had a picture in his mind of what the vehicle would look like. He now had to work out the details.

---

* For more information about spatial abilities in learning-disabled students, read *The Spatial Child* by John Dixon.

Mike devoted himself so thoroughly to his goal that it took precedence over all other activities. He first listed all the things he would need to complete the project. He then completed a carefully drawn, multicolored diagram of the complex inner wiring that would be required for his plan. Luckily his father was an electrician, so Mike was able to discuss his ideas with his dad as he planned the project. He also asked his dad to help him obtain the necessary materials.

All were in awe when Mike displayed his model vehicle. No longer was he the shy and insecure student described by his teachers and classmates. Rather he exuded confidence about his ability and pride in his achievement. Like Louis, he was a practicing professional whose performance was of an excellent quality.

It is useful to identify the self-regulatory behaviors that Mike employed in the pursuit of his goal. This is outlined in Table 6.7 below.

After Mike was finished with his project, he discussed with his mentor how he was able to accomplish his goal. Together they devised ways in which similar strategies that Mike could use to be more successful in the required school curriculum. Mike thought about picturing projects and concepts in his mind as the teacher described them. Perhaps instead of taking notes initially, he could tape the teacher's lecture and sketch out the ideas in a storyboard fashion. Another idea was to see a movie about the topic before it was discussed or even visit a museum or historical site related to the topic under discussion. Mike remembers how his parents had taken him to Gettysburg the summer before and how that visit made the concepts and details in the unit on the Civil War easy to grasp and remember. Mike realized that when he had the goal clearly pictured in his mind, it was easy to recall the details. It was like imagining a picture of an event with details missing. Reading the assignment and listening to the lecture then was a matter of filling in the missing pieces.

Table 6.7   Mike's Application of Self-Regulation Strategies

Self-Regulation Strategies	*Personal Applications*
Understanding what is required in the problem	Reading the material for specific details Creating a visual image of what the vehicle looks like
Goal setting	Sketching out model
Planning steps	Listing materials needed Setting due date Establishing a visual time line with steps listed and target dates estimated
Seeking feedback	Asking his dad for advice before initiating plan
Allocating time	Forgetting activities not absolutely necessary until project is done

Recall the story of Debra, our young historian described in Chapter 1. Early in the GLD program she attended, similar strategies were discovered, explored and articulated. These were the strategies she applied as she conducted her research study. Debra used mapping to organize her ideas (strategy for organization = visual mapping). She visited the Noah Webster House several times to remember details (strategy for memorizing details: repeated oral and visual exposure). She chose to assume the role of Jerusha Webster and to portray her life in a slide and tape presentation (strategy for communication = using her talent in dramatic expression). She asked if she could practice her narrative at home where there would be fewer distractions and where she could rehearse until she was proud of her effort (strategy for focusing attention = finding an environment where there were fewer distractions).

The scenarios described above show how an enrichment activity was used to help the students identify self-regulating behaviors that they employ when they are achieving in an area of strength and interest. However, because life requires sustained effort and the application of self-regulatory behaviors on far less exciting tasks, we must teach GLD students how to apply their brand of self-regulatory behaviors to the usual classroom fare such as studying for a test or memorizing the Periodic Chart. In Chapter 9, we discuss the use of strategies with more typical curriculum requirements.

The possibilities are endless for helping students to become their own advocates by putting them in charge of their own learning. However, as we have pointed out in this chapter, success depends upon understanding the natural learning strengths of these students and making them feel efficacious about their own learning abilities. You will find the WISC-R patterns to be a useful foundation to develop both enrichment and compensation strategies that accomplish these goals.

PART THREE
Practical Considerations

INTRODUCTION

In earlier sections of the book, we detailed the unique needs demonstrated by GLD students. It is apparent that they need both attention to their gift and help with their learning difficulties. The previous section provided important information that can be used in meeting the varied needs of this special population of students. In this final section we consider strategies for meeting these needs. There are three broad stages developed. First, strategies are needed to identify GLD students. Second, a program designed must be consistent with the needs of the population and with boundaries set by local considerations. Last, teachers must be made aware of curricular strategies and techniques that will enhance the learning and self-confidence of the students.

In Chapter 7, we emphasize ways to identify GLD students. The first part of the chapter presents general guidelines for identifying a learning disability. We describe both formal and informal procedures and provide sample assessment tools. The emphasis of this chapter is on identifying the gifts of students who are having difficulty learning. We discuss a variety of ways to document a youngster's potential for gifted behavior such as test scores, interview schedules and teacher observations of student behavior in creative and complex activities. Sample identification activities and observational checklists and assessment documents are shown.

Chapter 8 describes a variety of programs that are specifically designed to attend to the students' talents. First, general characteristics common to all these programs are described. For instance, most successful programs identify the students' strengths and develop programs that nurture that talent in its own right. The second part of the chapter considers the appropriateness of enrolling GLD students in existing gifted programs such as advanced placement courses or pullout enrichment programs. The chapter closes with descriptions of three programs that were specially designed for the GLD student: a mentorship program, a resource room program based on the Enrichment Triad Model (Renzulli, 1977), and a two phase enrichment program that involved a cooperative effort between the teacher of the gifted and the learning disability specialist.

The final chapter concentrates on teaching strategies that will enable GLD students to compensate for problematic weaknesses, to gain a more positive attitude about school and their individual abilities, and to become motivated to take charge of their learning. The strategies are divided into four categories. The first set of strategies included will help teachers select appropriate activities so that these students receive the sophisticated challenge they require. The second type of strategies provide the teacher with ideas for helping GLD students to compensate for problematic weaknesses. The next section offers suggestion for managing the inconsistent and often difficult learning behaviors of these students. The chapter concludes with directions for conducting rap sessions as a way of offering emotional support, plus resources to help them plan for their postsecondary education.

CHAPTER 7

IDENTIFICATION

The purpose of this chapter is to discuss a variety of strategies helpful in identifying GLD students. Because the definitions in both domains are characteristically inconsistent in the literature, this task may at first glance appear complex and tedious at best. However, it is our aim to provide procedures to simplify the identification process in a meaningful way.

Ultimately, the process in the identification of gifted, learning-disabled students involves obtaining evidence supporting the presence of a specific learning disability on the one hand, and the potential for giftedness on the other. The sequence of the process usually depends on which characteristics of the child first flag our attention (see Chapter 3). However, no matter which exceptionality becomes the primary diagnosis, it is exceedingly important not to ignore behaviors which may be indicative of the other.

In this chapter, first we will discuss general guidelines in identifying a learning disability, and then describe in greater detail the strategies for recognizing patterns of giftedness. The choice of this emphasis is the result of two factors. The first is that much has already been written on the identification of learning disabilities. Because we are not challenging the procedures that are already widely used, we will simply summarize them. The second reason is that teachers can easily detect when children are not achieving or when they are experiencing difficulty in learning (even though the underlying causes of poor achievement may be elusive to them). However, these same teachers are frequently at a loss when trying to find gifts in children who cannot read, write, compute or attend to tasks.

Procedures for Identification of a Specific Learning Disability

Identification begins when parents or teachers suspect that a student is having difficulty in the learning process. A referral initiates formal assessment procedures or "the process of gathering information for decision making" (Lewis & Doorlag, 1983) Both formal testing and observational analyses are used to collect data to document three areas of performance (see Chapter 2 for definition of LD):

1. Discrepancy between intellectual potential and academic performance,
2. Psychological processing difficulties, and
3. Learning behaviors.

Documentation of a Severe Discrepancy

Universally, learning disabilities represent a gap between what the child is expected to accomplish based on his intellectual abilities or IQ and what he is achieving. Because the term *discrepancy* is somewhat vague and ambiguous, some states have sought to aid clarity by suggesting the use of a formula to indicate the degree of severity. Ohio, for instance, requires that a child's IQ score be two standard deviations above their composite score on an achievement test. For example, if a child had an IQ of 130 and this child's achievement score in a particular area (math) were at the fiftieth percentile, this achievement percentile would be the equivalent of an IQ of 100. This would mean that there would be an IQ difference of thirty points (130—100). Since the standard deviation on most IQ tests is fifteen points, this thirty point discrepancy would represent two standard deviations. The child would qualify on the basis of the discrepancy scores. It is important to note that this cannot be the sole criterion according to Federal Law. This is only one guide to identifying LD children.* Individual intelligence tests and achievement tests are primarily used to assess cognitive ability and academic achievement levels. Table 7.1 lists those tests frequently used.

Evaluating Psychological Processing Difficulties

Definitions of learning disabilities strongly imply that discrepancies between potential and performance are due to problems in how students perceive or process information. Tests again provide information on such neuro-psychological processes. Popular tests are also recorded in Table 7.1.

Learning Behavior Assessment

Behavioral characteristics of learning-disabled students historically have been important in distinguishing LD students from non-LD. Typical characteristics cited in the literature include hyperactivity, mood shifts, general coordination deficits, impulsiveness, short attention span, acting-out or withdrawn behavior, distractibility, and low self-esteem. Although some norm-referenced behavioral scales are available to document these characteristics, we feel that informal techniques are more informative and practical. Anecdotal observations, teacher-rating scales, and samples of student's work give important information about students' learning behaviors.

When informal observation and anecdotal information provide examples of characteristic behaviors, it is important to note the frequency of the behavior, whether it corroborates test information, and whether the behavior interferes with the student's classroom performance. On pages 59 and 60 are two examples of informal teacher information taken from *Ohio Guidelines for Identification of Children with Specific Learning Disabilities* published by the State of Ohio Department of Education.

A diagnosis of specific learning disability can be made after careful consideration of both formal and informal information as well as documentation of the severity of the disability.

Unfortunately, many states will not consider a learning problem unless achievement is at least a year below grade level. For very bright children who are having learning problems, this creates a major problem. Often such children are performing at grade level when, in fact, estimates of their ability predict superior performance. This blatant underachievement could be due to a subtle learning disability. However, this discrepancy will probably be ignored because the student is achieving at grade level, and thus ineligible for supportive services.

Professionals working with bright students must ignore such policies when considering appropriate programs for gifted but disabled students. Indeed, for some of these bright youngsters, finding a reason why certain tasks remain so difficult for them despite focused effort gives them proof that they are not lazy or crazy. They can finally understand that inconsistencies in performance have a neurological basis. Furthermore, they can then be made aware of strategies available to help them overcome or circumvent individual weaknesses.

Table 7.1　Tests Typically Used to Assess Learning Disabilities

Intellectual Functioning	Academic Achievement	Psychological Processing
Wechsler Intelligence Scale for Children-Revised (Wechsler, 1974) (Verbal & Performance Abilities)	Peabody Individual Achievement (Dunn & Markwardt 1970). (Math, Reading, Recognition, Reading Comprehension, Spelling and General Information) (Markwardt, 1989) Wide Range Achievement Test (Jastak & Wilkinson, 1989) Brigance (Inventory of Basic Skills) Key Math (Connolly, 1988) Durrell Reading Test (Durrell & Catterson, 1980) Slosson Reading (Slosson & Richardson, 1990)	Motor-Free Visual Perception Test (Colarusso & Hammil, 1972) Auditory Discrimination Test (Wepman, 1975) Goldman-Fristoe-Woodcock Auditory Skills Test Battery (Goldman, Fristoe, & Wood-cock, 1976) Detroit Tests of Learning Aptitude (2) (Hammil, 1985)

* For a more detailed explanation of the discrepancy formula, the reader can send for *LD Discrepancy Formula: A Handbook*, prepared by C.F. Telzrow and J.L. Williams. It is available from Cuyahoga Special Education Service Center, 14605 Granger Road, Maple Heights, OH 44137.

Primary/Intermediate Teacher Checklist of Suspected SLD Student Characteristics

Student:_____ Date of Birth:_____

Teacher:_____

Date:_____

Subject/Grade:_____

	Most of the time	Some of the time	Seldom	Never	Not observed
1. Finishes things begun					
2. Listens attentively					
3. Concentrates on schoolwork					
4. Thinks before acting					
5. Completes one activity before moving to another					
6. Organizes work appropriately					
7. Needs little supervision					
8. Waits turn in games or group situations					
9. Sits in seat without difficulty					
10. Demonstrates a good memory					
11. Follows and understands class discussions					
12. Adapts to new situations and locations appropriately					
13. Shows good judgement in social situations					
14. Cooperates without adult encouragement					
15. Is sought out by peers					
16. Does acceptable classwork in comparison to others					
17. Does acceptable classwork in comparison to ability					

Comments:_____

_____

_____

Educational Recommendation:_____

_____

_____

Attach Work Sheets

From Ohio Guidelines for the Identification of Children with Specific Learning Disabilities

Secondary Teacher Checklist of Suspected SLD Student Characteristics

Student:_____ Date of Birth:_____

Teacher:_____

Date:_____

Subject/Grade:_____

	Most of the time	Some of the time	Seldom	Never	Not observed
1. Arrives for class on time					
2. Brings necessary work materials to class					
3. Initiates work after directions are given					
4. Hands assignments in on time					
5. Does assignments neatly and in a readable manner					
6. Can organize materials logically (notebooks, assignments)					
7. Can maintain a notebook					
8. Can make notes independently from a lecture					
9. Can outline or take notes from a textbook					
10. Can handle more than one direction at a time					
11. Gets along well with adults					
12. Gets along well with peers					
13. Participates in class discussion/activities					
14. Accepts responsibility					
15. Demonstrates sound judgement					
16. Demonstrates self-discipline					
17. Demonstrates a good memory					

Comments:_____

_____

_____

Educational Recommendation:_____

_____

_____

Attach Work Sheets

From Ohio Guidelines for the Identification of Children with Specific Learning Disabilities

Procedures for Identification of the Gift

How do we recognize potential for gifted behavior in students who are learning disabled? In Chapter 2, we describe Renzulli's (1978) conception of creative productive giftedness as an interaction of three clusters of traits: well-above-average ability, creativity, and task commitment brought to bear upon a specific interest or field of endeavor. Renzulli, *et al.* (1981) further state that while ability estimates are mostly stable, creativity and task commitment may be situational or environmental. With learning-disabled students, it is most likely that evidence of traits will be found by exploring the student's total environment under both positive and negative circumstances, not by merely assessing behaviors on school-related tasks.

In addition, traditional strategies and preset attitudes will impede the identification of potential gifts in learning-disabled students. For instance, a total IQ score on a WISC-R will most likely underestimate the intellectual potential of a learning-disabled student. Rather, an analysis of subtest patterns will provide a more accurate picture of the student's conceptual abilities. This will be discussed more fully below. Likewise, some observed behaviors of learning-disabled students, like twenty-five reasons for not handing in homework or a preoccupation with a consuming interest, should sometimes be considered signs of creativity and task commitment rather than irresponsible or avoidance behaviors.

We generally approach the identification process in two ways. The first, which we call *a priori* identification, entails collecting and analyzing test data and interview information about students based on information already available. The second, which we refer to as dynamic identification involves using activities purposely designed to elicit creative responses and alert observers to possible areas of student talent and interests. The purpose of both approaches is to obtain evidence of well-above-average ability, creativity and task commitment in areas of students' strengths.

A Priori Identification

Using Test Scores. The initiatives of Lewis Terman have guided the development of gifted education for many years. One of the legacies coming from Terman was a strong emphasis on using intelligence tests as the basis for determining which children are gifted and which are not. This is still a dominant feature of gifted education programs in many communities. This approach has come under considerable criticism in recent years, and justly so, because intelligence tests are consistently found to be weak predictors of the adult accomplishments of gifted people. In other words, while the possession of above-average intelligence on an IQ test may be the indication of the possibility of significant accomplishment, there are so many intellectually capable people who do little with their abilities and others who through sheer effort overcome deficiencies, that there is bound to be a low association between measured intelligence and accomplishment. One implication of this is that IQ tests should not be relied on as a basis for determining the giftedness of children.

While we agree entirely that this sort of evidence should be taken as a caution against exclusive reliance on IQ testing, the other side of this argument is that performance on an IQ test is one carefully controlled sampling of a child's performance. This sampling should never be taken as a definitive indicator of a child's potential, but we have found IQ information as a valuable starting point for getting a hint of what a child might do in further challenging situations. The important thing is not to over-select on the basis of IQ information before other information has been looked at. For one thing, IQ criteria should not be set so high that other information becomes irrelevant. Likewise, the diagnostician should not become fixated on IQ information just because it might be the first information collected. It is just one of several sources of information—but a potentially valuable one.

In addition to being one sampling, good IQ information can also tell a valuable story about the particular strength and weakness patterns common among GLD children. This will only be the case if the IQ test employed has a valuable assortment of subtests within which the strength and weakness patterns can be observed. Since the IQ test most widely employed with learning-disabled children is the WISC-R, this is usually not a problem.

Interpreting the WISC-R. When looking at WISC-R scores, the most important thing is to look for areas of distinct strength which are logically connected. In doing this, one might use the subtest categories suggested in Chapter 6. For example, if a child has high scores on all three of the spatial manipulation subtests (Block Design, Object Assembly, and Picture Completion), this could be an indication of talent in this particular area. On the other hand, one should not be overly focused on these particular categories. For example, the tests in the Patterned Sequencing subtests will tend to correlate very strongly with the Spatial Manipulation Subtests, so a combination of strengths in the two areas is a very logical possibility. The important thing is that there be a conceptual foundation to the strength pattern one is observing. Any child of average intelligence is likely to have two or more subtests which are somewhat above average. If one allows a random selection of subtests to be the basis of asserting that there is a strength, many children will be identified on the basis of normal random test score variation. One should be able to say exactly what the area of strength is, or it is possible that there is none.

It is important not to let the areas of weakness prevent one from asserting that there is a strength. It is not at all unusual for GLD children to have particular subtest scores which are one or more standard deviations below the mean. This should be expected and not hinder the assertion of a talent.

Most of the time the talents of the GLD child will be manifested across the Integrative Intelligence areas (Spatial Manipulation, Patterned Sequencing, and Abstract Conceptualization) with one or another of these areas being slightly stronger. The weaknesses of these children are most likely to be in the Dispersive Intelligence areas (Detailed Memory, Quick Information Processing and Patternless Sequencing). More often than not, this broader distinction will be the basis of identifying the talent.

In looking for the difference between Integrative Intelligence and Dispersive Intelligence, one should be careful not to shift over into the distinction between verbal and performance tests (and discrepancies) just because test information is often reported in these terms. The strengths of GLD children often cross the line between verbal and performance scores and their weaknesses also often cross this line. The verbal-performance discrepancy will, therefore, muddle the true discrepancies which can be found.

In order to make this point clear, let us look at the example of a WISC-R score pattern in Figure 7.2 on the next page. Most impressive is the Object Assembly score of 19, but also the Block Design score of 15, the Picture Arrangement score of 14, the Comprehension score of 15, and the Vocabulary score of 15. Also, the Similarities score is somewhat elevated at 13. The strengths of this child appear across the areas of Integrative Intelligence. On the other hand, the weaknesses are in the area of Dispersive Intelligence—Arithmetic 7, Coding 8, and Digit Span 9. If in evaluating the discrepancies for this child, the scores from the Verbal tests had been lumped together, and those from the Performance test had been lumped together, the discrepancy between these two areas would appear as rather unimpressive. Identifying the discrepancy in that way would violate the clarity that can be achieved through other distinctions. This particular child would appear to be quite spatial and somewhat abstract.

If identification were based on either a full scale IQ score, or on the Verbal IQ score of the Performance IQ score, this child would not look very distinguished or interesting. The Full Scale score was 114, the Verbal was 107, and the Performance, 120.

In looking at this test pattern, the question might be raised as to how high test scores need to be in order to be considered indications of talent. The rule of thumb from our experience is that in the area of defined strength, the child will have scaled scores of 13 or above with at least one or two being 15 or more. This meets the Renzulli criterion of showing distinctly above-average ability, while not putting the standard so high that children with strong motivational and unusual creative potential will be eliminated before being able to demonstrate these other sides of the mix.

Using a Structured Interview. Once well-above-average intellectual ability has been documented, information about task commitment, interests and creativity can be collected. One way to seek out these behaviors is to use a structured interview with adults who are well acquainted with the students. The one on page 65 was adapted from items on Scales for Rating the Behavioral Characteristics of Superior Students (Renzulli *et al.*, 1976). The learning disability resource room teacher provided the information. From this interview, we

WISC-R RECORD FORM

Wechsler Intelligence Scale
for Children—Revised

NAME_____AGE_____SEX_____
ADDRESS_____
PARENTS NAME_____
SCHOOL_____GRADE_____
PLACE OF TESTING_____TESTED BY_____
REFERRED BY_____

WISC-R PROFILE

Clinicians who wish to draw a profile should first transfer the child's scaled scores to the row of boxes below. Then mark an X on the dot corresponding to the scaled score for each test, and draw a line connecting the X's.

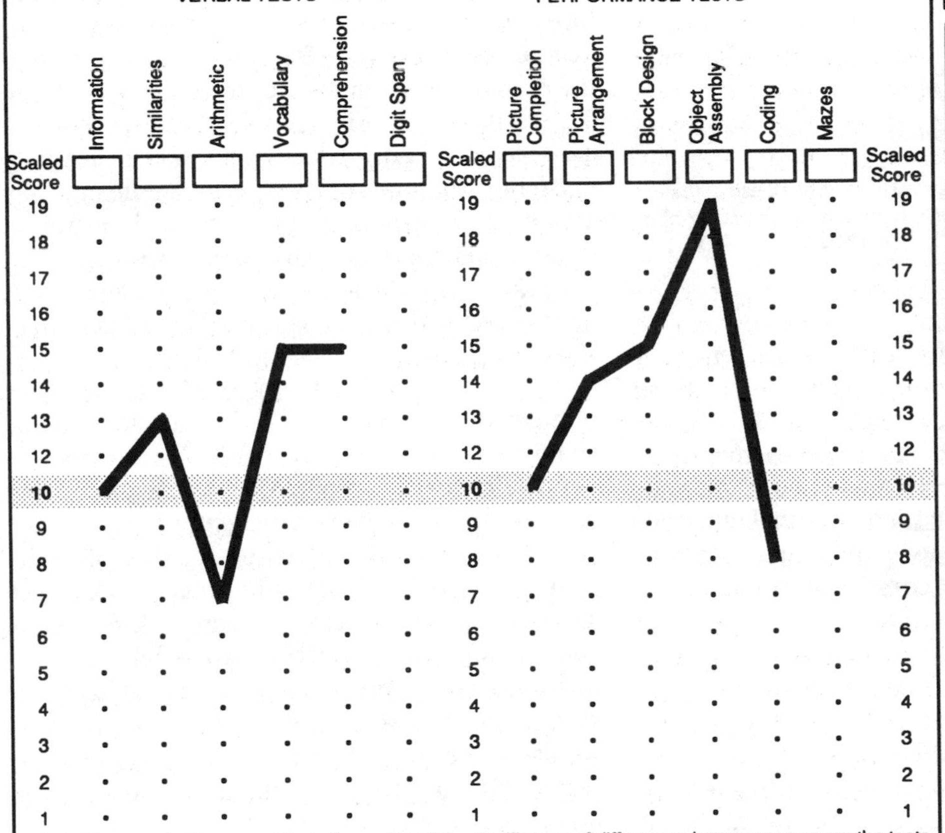

	Year	Month	Day
Date Tested			
Date of Birth			
Age			

VERBAL TESTS — Information, Similarities, Arithmetic, Vocabulary, Comprehension, Digit Span

PERFORMANCE TESTS — Picture Completion, Picture Arrangement, Block Design, Object Assembly, Coding, Mazes

	Raw Score	Scaled Score
VERBAL TESTS		
Information		10
Similarities		13
Arithmetic		7
Vocabulary		15
Comprehension		15
(Digit Span)	( )	( )
Verbal Score		107
PERFORMANCE TESTS		
Picture Completion		10
Picture Arrangement		14
Block Design		15
Object Assembly		19
Coding		8
(Mazes)	( )	( )
Performance Score		120

	Scaled Score	IQ
Verbal Score		*107
Performance Score		*120
Full Scale Score		114

* Prorated from 4 tests, if necessary.

* See Chapter 4 in the manual for a discussion of the significance of differences between scores on the tests.

NOTES

Figure 7.2   GLC Student's Profile of Abilities

have learned a great deal about the strengths of this student. This information, along with his profile on the WISC-R, confirms most positively his potential for gifted behavior. (See Appendix D for blank form.)

Well above average ability
1. WISC-R profile (subtest scores)
2. Understanding and interest in adult topics
3. Knowledge of history
4. Inquisitive mind, questioning everything
5. Authored plays with complicated plots and many characters

Creativity
1. Had a lot of excuses (fluency)
2. Clever avoider
3. Inquisitive mind
4. Imaginative stories, wrote a play
5. Sees humor in situations

Task commitment
1. Passion for history—learned a great deal of history on his own.
2. Reads all books on history. (Notice he does not read well in a traditional sense, but studies print material in area of interest. This is typical behavior of GLD students.)
3. Spends much time absorbed in books in interest area.

Indeed, adults who are not sensitive to behaviors indicative of giftedness might view this child as clever, irresponsible, and manipulative. It is imperative to view learning characteristics, however, from an objective perspective where one does not evaluate a particular behavior on original intent but rather views the behavior as an intellectual strength which, if redirected, can contribute to the child's ability to become a productive adult.

Dynamic Identification

Both Tannenbaum (1983) and Renzulli (1978) assert that to identify potential for giftedness in students we must expose them to and instruct them in particular domains. Then we must assess their ability, interest, creativity and commitment to the specific field or area of human endeavor. This is in fact the model used by athletic programs to identify and develop athletic talent in youngsters.

It is important to define first the kinds of abilities being sought and then to develop corresponding activities to use for identification. The results of open-ended, creative activities using a wide variety of experiences are excellent indicators of potential giftedness. Whole group lessons, center activities,

visitations, guest speakers and exploratory activities offer fine opportunities to recognize student enthusiasm, a passion for a topic, strengths and possible talents. The crucial component, however, is the ability of the teacher to notice the potential. Teachers must observe student behaviors during and after these experiences, particularly noting problem-solving abilities, leadership, original ideas, in-depth questions, elaborate products, and a desire to do more, go further, or continue with the activity or specific topic. Sometimes checklists to document behaviors as they occur are useful.

We have used dynamic identification in a number of programs for GLD students. In one such program, we sought to identify LD students who demonstrated potential for gifted behavior in spatial design, visual thinking or dramatic expression. We designed specific activities corresponding to each domain and instructed teachers in learning disability resource rooms how to use them. They administered the activities to all their learning-disabled students and rated their performance using behavioral checklists that we provided. Because we have found that these children often express their gift through spatial, visual, or dramatic expression, the activities are designed to tap intellectual strengths through these modes. Following are the sample activities and corresponding checklists.

The checklist on page 78 corresponds to behaviors important in dramatic expression.

The dynamic identification activities here described are some examples of creative options to offer these students. Activities can be developed in any specific domain, such as experimentation and inquiry activities in the hard sciences as well as the social sciences. Remember to offer a variety of hands-on activities in which the ability to read or write will not interfere with the child's performance.

Ideally, identification should include both *a priori* (WISC-R profile and structured interview) and dynamic information. *A priori* information is usually sufficient to document potential for gifted behavior. However, when trying to understand specific talents and areas in which these students are most comfortable, thinking and communicating dynamic information is especially useful. Dynamic information also identifies students who may not test well or students whose gifts are not easily measured by existing tests.

STRUCTURED INTERVIEW

1. Describe this child's interests.

   History (Civil War and other wars), does not read well, but learned a great deal of history. Sports.

2. Have you observed situations in which this child
   - becomes totally absorbed in a particular subject area?

   History. He reads all books on history, biography and on various periods and eras. He spends time absorbed in these books. No school subject interests him as much. Science is another strong interest. Any verbal discussion absorbs him as long as he does not have to write anything down.

   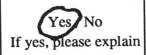

   - has discussed adult topics such as politics, religion, or current events?

   Yes, all of them. Everything was a topic of discussion for him. (For example, his father's college reunion.) He is interested in all adult topics, enjoys discussing them with adults and even asks adults about their own lives.

   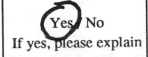

   - becomes self-assertive, stubborn or aggressive?

   Stubborn when he had to turn in a hard assignment. He had a lot of excuses and a lot of righteous-wounded indignation if you did not accept his excuses.

   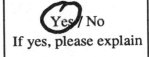

   - avoided tasks?

   Ditto as above. Everything involved with his LD he would avoid. He had all sorts of excuses: his dog died, his mother took him out, etc. Very clever avoider (for things he found hard to do).

   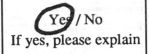

   - was particularly curious?

   He has an inquisitive mind, questioned everything and asked many times, "Why do you think such and such is so?"

   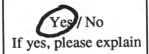

   - was highly imaginative?

   Yes. His written (or dictated to LD teacher) stories revealed his imagination. He would talk these stories then shorten them and put them on paper. They had complicated plots and many characters. He also wrote a play.

   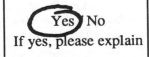

   - was humorous or seemed to be aware of nuances of humor?

   A crooked smile. When you saw that smile, you knew he was getting the humor of the situation. Even his excuses were funny and he said them with humor.

   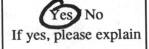

   For each item, circled: Yes / No — "If yes, please explain"

Gifts in Spatial Design

Activities in spatial design involve building or creating in three dimensional space. Following are some activities we have found successful in locating students whose gift is expressed through spatial experiences. Participation in the Odyssey of the Mind™ program afford these students both an opportunity to be identified and an opportunity to use their talents in an exciting challenge.

Activity I

Materials needed: Legos™ or other building materials; who, what, and where cards arranged in three stacks, face down. Sample cards may be similar to the following:

Who	*What*	*Where*
George Washington	House	In Atlantis
Larry Bird	Hideaway	On the moon
Mickey Mouse	Radio	Under a mushroom
Chris Everet	Desk	In a tree
The President	Vehicle	At the South Pole
E.T.	Playground	On a cloud
Romeo	Office	In Mexico

Procedure: Explain to the students that they are expert engineers and have been hired to design a variety of new creations. They can work individually or in groups. To receive their special assignment, they are to choose one card from each of the stacks. Their product will be judged on how well the creation accommodates the character's personal needs, and how the object reflects the environmental considerations as well.

Example: Suppose a student selected the cards Mickey Mouse, Vehicle, and On the moon. The student would then have to create some sort of vehicle that would be designed for Mickey and be able to operate successfully on the moon. Note that knowledge, creativity and building ability are all necessary to complete a superior product. Students gifted in spatial design will use the bricks to build wonderful objects and include many details showing their knowledge of the subjects involved. They might, for example, design a vehicle for Mickey Mouse on the moon might need some sort of trap avoider, cheese storage bin, a gravity creator, and so on. They will consult references to help them fill in important details as needed. In this case, they might consult comic books or a Disney anthology to check what Mickey's hobbies are. They might also find out whether Mickey usually drives or prefers Minnie to do the driving. In summary, their findings will be reflected in the details of the finished project.

Activity 2

Scienceworks
Ontario Science Center

THE next time you see a house or a high-rise under construction, look at the shapes made by the frame. Some shapes are stronger than others. You don't need steel girders to experiment with shapes. You can raid the kitchen for building materials.

You'll need:
a package of toothpicks
miniature marshmallows (or modeling clay)
a hardcover book
2 chairs
5 quarters in a paper cup

1. Using the toothpicks as beams and the marshmallows (or balls of modeling clay) as glue, try to build a tall structure using nine marshmallows and 15 toothpicks.
2. Now try building with 15 marshmallows and nine toothpicks. Which structure is stronger? When you look at the stronger one, do you see more triangles?
3. Using 14 marshmallows and 20 toothpicks, try to make a structure that's strong enough to hold the book.
4. Here's a final challenge: Try building a bridge between two chairs 30 cm (1 foot) apart. Use as many marshmallows and toothpicks as necessary. When you're done, see if it will hold the cup full of quarters.

Note: If you want to make bigger, stronger and more permanent structures, attach toothpicks with glue instead of marshmallows.

Ontario Science Center, *Scienceworks*, © 1984, by Centennial Centre of Science and Technology, pp.70, 71. Reprinted with permission of Addison-Wesly Publishing Company, Inc., Reading, MA.

Activity 3

Scienceworks
Ontario Science Center

AVE you ever watched a house being built? Under the bricks or siding, there's a frame of wooden beams—the skeleton of the house. The frame gives the building its strength. It's not difficult to build a frame that would hold up a house. Test your construction skills by building with beams make of newspaper.

You'll Need:
sheets of old newspaper (make sure everyone has read them!
toothpicks
tape

1. Lay a sheet of newspaper flat on the floor. Place a toothpick across one corner and roll the newspaper tightly around the toothpick until the whole sheet is rolled. Fasten it with the tape. If you've rolled tightly enough, you'll have a long, strong, newspaper dowel that is very hard to bend. (If you want to shorten it, cut off the ends.)

2. Repeat the above process until you have a pile of newspaper beams.

3. When you're ready to start building, attach the beams together with tape. Start by outlining the shape of your building on the floor, using the beams. Then build up.

4. As you build, you might have to brace your frame with crossbeams.

5. Build your building as high as you can. Can you make it reach the ceiling?

Talent Identification

Child's Name: _____

Classroom Teacher: _____

	Evidence				
	None	Some	Average	Above Avg.	Exceptional
Above average ability					
Comprehension: "I get it," I see possibilities.					
Independence: asks for little guidance					
Tool use: experienced with tools and materials					
learns quickly					
Focus: follows a plan in his/her head					
Speed: quantity of detail					
Integration: project works					
Creativity					
Changes scope of problem					
Uses materials in unique ways					
Adds new materials					
Adapts, finds materials					
Balance, symmetry [or]					
Bold, risk-taking elements					
Task commitment					
Enthusiasm: "I like building."					
Integration: finishes project					
Troubleshooting: solves own problems					
Reports additional work					
Discusses other possibilities					

Adapted from Bill Brown
Creative Arts Workshop, New Haven, CT

Gifts in Visual Literacy

by Linda Emerick

For students who are visually-oriented (two-dimensional) activities in film making are particularly appropriate for identifying creative talent. It is important to note that students talented in this domain do not necessarily have to be visual artists, but rather they have an extraordinary ability and preference to use a visual mode to solve problems, remember details, and organize and generate ideas. The book, *Visual Thinking* (McKinnon, 1980) provides an excellent overview of this way of representing and understanding knowledge. We have included below some exploratory activities in film making that you might use with students to determine their abilities as visual thinkers. For additional information on film, storyboarding, and other photographic techniques, we suggest the following sources:

Brodbeck, E. (1975). *Handbook of basic motion picture technique.* NY: Amphoto.

Gaskill, A.L. & Englander, D.A. (1985). *How to shoot a movie and video story.* Dobbs Ferry, NY: Morgan & Morgan, Inc.

Laybourne, K. (1979). *The animation book.* NY: Crown Publishing.

Levine, P., Glasser, J. & Gach, S. (1984). *The complete guide to home video production.* NY: Crown Publishing.

Titelman, C. (1979). *The art of Star Wars.* NY: Ballentine Books.

Following the exploratory activities is a behavioral checklist that you may use to evaluate superior ability demonstrated by students as they complete the activities.

Lesson I: What Do We Really See on TV?

Concepts to introduce:
1. Scenes on the screen are made up of *shots*.
2. Shots can vary in length.
3. There are different kinds of shots based on cinematographic techniques.
4. The length and type of shots used affect the viewer's emotions and feelings about the subject.

What is a "shot"?
1. Give a definition of this term.
2. Give several examples. It may be useful to use a video or other camera to indicate when a shot begins and ends.
3. Using a TV or film, practice counting shots with students.
4. Ask for ideas concerning why a director or editor would choose to use shots which are long or short in length.
5. For those who are interested:

Watch 30 minutes of your favorite prime-time action TV show. Count all the shots (do not include commercials). Keep a tally sheet and bring the total to class to compare shows and for further discussion.

How are shots different?

1. Using drawings or other examples, illustrate how different kinds of shots can affect our feelings and opinions.
2. Introduce:

   Close-up   High angle
   Medium shot   Low angle
   Long shot

3. Ask students to share examples they may remember (for example, Darth Vader is always low angle).
4. Using TV film, call out shots and encourage students to do the same. Commercials are great for this activity.
5. Discuss *why* these choices may have been made.

Lesson II: Creating a Storyboard

Concepts to introduce:

1. Planning is necessary to transfer an idea to a visual image.
2. Storyboards are used in planning.
3. Variety of shots, length of shots is used to create interest.

What is a storyboard?

1. Show examples of storyboards (professional, students). (See references.)
2. Discuss how types of shots used have unique impact.

Activity: Complete the storyboard (group) See Activity #1
Activity: Change the mood (individual). See Activity #2.

Lesson III: Special Effects (SP-FX)

Concepts to introduce:

1. Much of what is viewed on TV or in the movies is not real.
2. There are many types of "tricks" the camera can do.
3. SP-FX are a form of problem-solving.

Types of SP-FX

1. Give at least two examples of SP-FX (animation, slow motion are easily understood by most children).
2. Ask students to share examples of what they consider SP-FX in shows they have viewed.

Analyzing a SP-FX

1. Show a storyboard treatment of a SP-FX. Discuss each shot with the class.
2. Show another storyboard. Ask students for their analysis.

Activity: SP-FX problem

SP-FX Problems

1. We have run into a problem with the film, "A Life for a Friend." One scene calls for a rock to explode into many pieces when aliens give a demonstration of their power. We cannot use explosives or real rocks because of the safety threat. Using only materials available in the school, how might the illusion of an exploding rock be created for film?

2. The third graders are having some difficulty with a scene in their action-adventure video production. The heroine is supposed to slip over the edge of a tall building and them crawl back to safety. Mrs. Brady is not excited about the thought of her daughter dangling from a real building. The third graders have the following materials and would like your ideas concerning a solution. Keep in mind that we do not want the actress more than 10 inches above the ground—or the camera person.

   A. Large sheets of cardboard
   B. Tempera paint and brushes
   C. Desks
   D. Chairs
   E. Standard school-type materials

3. The group making the spoof of *Raiders of the Lost Ark* have a very tricky problem that needs work. One scene depicts the hero (Wisconsin Smith) attempting to swing across a deep pit using his whip which is wrapped around an overhead branch. Unfortunately, the group reports there is no pit, no tree, and they don't want to cut this scene because of the humor involved. Any ideas how this action can be depicted?

Aliens from "A Life for a Friend"

1981

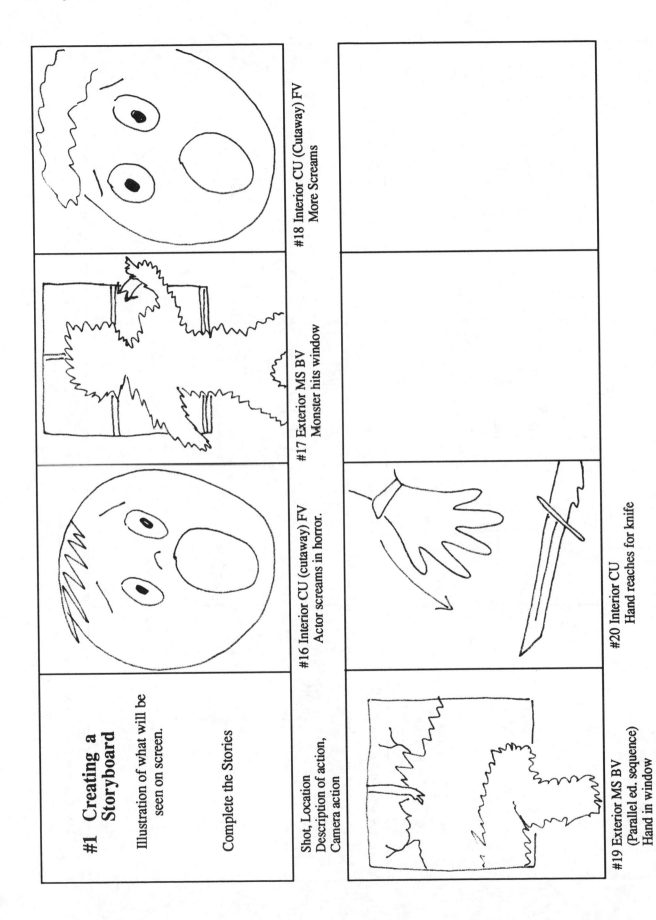

#1   Creating a Storyboard

Illustration of what will be seen on screen.

Complete the Stories

Shot, Location
Description of action,
Camera action

#16 Interior CU (cutaway) FV
Actor screams in horror.

#17 Exterior MS BV
Monster hits window

#18 Interior CU (Cutaway) FV
More Screams

#19 Exterior MS BV
(Parallel ed. sequence)
Hand in window

#20 Interior CU
Hand reaches for knife

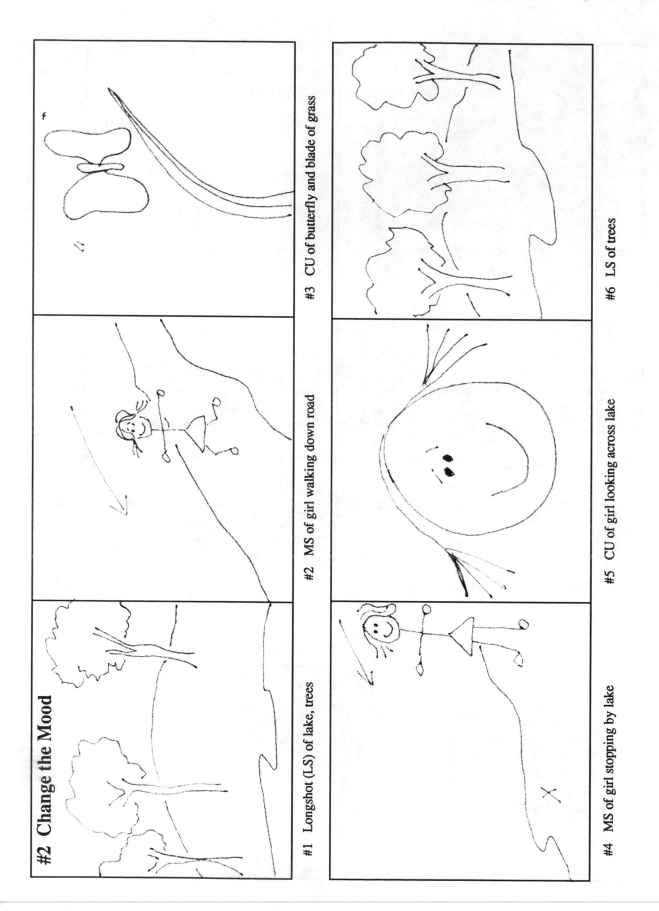

#2 Change the Mood

#1 Longshot (LS) of lake, trees

#2 MS of girl walking down road

#3 CU of butterfly and blade of grass

#4 MS of girl stopping by lake

#5 CU of girl looking across lake

#6 LS of trees

Characteristics Checklist

L. Emerick, 1985

	Rarely	Sometimes	Often	Almost Always
Interest, Attitude				
1. Participates in activities eagerly	_____	_____	_____	_____
2. Impatient with others who show confusion, disinterest	_____	_____	_____	_____
3. Body movement, posture indicate high degree of interest	_____	_____	_____	_____
4. Expresses an "outside" interest in the topic	_____	_____	_____	_____
5. Expresses a desire to learn more	_____	_____	_____	_____
Above-average Ability				
1. Grasps concepts quickly	_____	_____	_____	_____
2. Gives example related to concepts	_____	_____	_____	_____
3. Asks questions that seek *depth* of information	_____	_____	_____	_____
4. Enjoys trying to solve complex problems	_____	_____	_____	_____
5. Evaluates, analyzes examples	_____	_____	_____	_____
Creativity				
1. Has unique solutions to problems	_____	_____	_____	_____
2. Sketches, draws in addition to or instead of verbalizing ideas	_____	_____	_____	_____
3. Manipulates, elaborates ideas	_____	_____	_____	_____
4. Generates many ideas and possible solutions	_____	_____	_____	_____
5. Can visualize scenes from different perspectives	_____	_____	_____	_____
Task Commitment				
1. Can concentrate for long periods of time	_____	_____	_____	_____
2. Asks questions or gives examples *after* instruction has been completed	_____	_____	_____	_____
3. Is not easily frustrated when involved with a task	_____	_____	_____	_____
4. Concerned with clarity, quality of product	_____	_____	_____	_____
5. Can organize ideas well	_____	_____	_____	_____
6. Indicates lasting interest	_____	_____	_____	_____

Additional comments:

Identification Activities in Dramatic Expression

by Gail Herman

As mentioned earlier, some GLD students excel in areas that require dramatic expression. Cher and Tom Cruz are excellent examples of dyslexic individuals whose salvation is the dramatic arts. The activities described below will help you to identify your future Academy Award winners. Again, we have provided an observational checklist to help you document and evaluate the performance of your students.

Wave Craze: To spot students who can develop different characters.

Students are to form a circle. The teacher or first person waves hello to the second person and says, "Hi" or "Hello" or some other greeting. The second person repeats the exact same gesture, body stance and tone of voice as the teacher's . Then the second student turns to the third student and waves hello using a totally different gesture and movement style. Continue around the circle, each person mimicking one person's gesture and then creating a totally different gesture for the next person to mimic. One goal is not to repeat any of the characters created. Then allow students to volunteer after the second round.

Teachers should be able to spot students who could imitate characters as well as create their own characters by using different body stances, voices, and gestures. Teachers should be able to spot students who can elaborate and focus on the activity without attending to any chance distractions.

Chick-A-Boom: To spot students who can "try on" a variety of voices using the call and echo structure.

Leader: Chick-a-boom, chick-a-boom (said in a character voice)
Group: Chick-a-boom, chick-a-boom (said in a character voice)
Leader: Repeat with slightly different emphasis, *e.g.,* emphasize the "boom."
Group: Repeats the leader's emphasis.
Leader: Chick-a-rocka, chick-a-rocka, chick-a-rocka, chick-a-boom!
Group: Repeats a leader's words and manner.

The leader continues to lead the chant but changes character voices. The leader also explains the usefulness of changing pitch (high-low tones); volume (loud-soft); inflection (patterns of rising and falling tones which create meaning and accents); quality (raspy, thin, smooth, deep). These contrasts help listeners to identify different characters. Students are invited to become leaders after the activity is established by the leader. Any group of phrases or sentences can be substituted for "chick-a-boom" if desired.

Teachers can spot students who are able to create character voices or who have a wide range of vocal variety. Also teachers may note that some students use their whole bodies when they are leading the group. This should be encouraged because the voice is the result of the emotional impulse within which feeling is often displayed through body movements and facial expression. Through this activity, teachers should also be able to spot students who have ability to create moods and motives for characters.

King of This Land: To spot students who can create full characters and character voices and movements.

Students form a circle. One person enters the circle and says, "I am King (or Queen) of this land." The statement is repeated several times with eye contact and vocal variations on word emphasis. The student walks in a small circle inside the larger circle. Then the teacher taps a willing second person from the circle who taps the first King on the shoulder and says, "Excuse me, but there must be some mistake. I am King (or Queen) of this land." The first person goes back to the big circle taking the second person's spot. The game continues. Each new King or Queen creates a new royal character (behaves with nobility, firmness or with great poise).

Teachers can spot students who participate with enthusiasm, who volunteer, capture the group's attention when speaking or "hamming it up" or who display exceptional poise. Teachers should notice those who use facial expression easily, those who have a large number of original ideas, or move easily in character.

Teachers can also ask students to create an improvisation with two clowns who meet and discover they are both hired by the circus thinking they were the ONLY clown. The improvisation is their meeting, and each clown's goal is to convince the other clown to leave. The game can be played with other characters such as space alien, goblin, etc.

Story Spoon: To spot students with strengths in storytelling and characterization.

The group uses a spoon to signify the storyteller for a sentence. The teacher might begin by saying, "Once upon a time, there lived a little chipmunk who became lost." Or, "Justin did not realize he was lost when he headed back in his Corvette." Each person adds a sentence to build on the previous ones. Stress fluency of ideas. A helpful technique for beginners is to repeat part of the last sentence which helps lead into an extended or different idea.

For groups of students who only add violent ideas upon violent ideas, stop and do a "FFOE" check (fluency, flexibility, originality, and elaboration). With the students, list on the board the various ideas developed. If the only category is violence, a rut has been developed. Ruts prevent creative thinking. Challenge them to develop flexibility.

The Creative Dramatic Expression Checklist follows. Teachers can use it as a guide to record student's behavior. The student's name can be jotted down next to the items which that student displayed during the identification activities each day.

Creative Dramatic Expression Checklist

Student's Name _____

School _____   Teacher _____

Phone _____   Class _____

(If observing a larger group, note the names of students displaying *outstanding* behavior next to the particular behavior.) Please check those that apply for each lesson.

	Rarely	Sometimes	Often	Almost Always
Above Average Ability				
1. Speaks clearly, or has a unique voice which attracts listeners	___	___	___	___
2. Uses gesture to augment words	___	___	___	___
3. Uses the whole body to develop characters	___	___	___	___
4. Movements to music indicate expressive interpretation	___	___	___	___
5. Can imitate or mimic other people's walks, voices, attitudes	___	___	___	___
6. Captures a group's attention when speaking by "hamming" or using exceptional poise	___	___	___	___
7. Uses facial expression	___	___	___	___
8. Can create a character	___	___	___	___
Creativity				
1. Offers a large number of ideas	___	___	___	___
2. Creates a wide variety of movement responses	___	___	___	___
3. Creates different kinds of characters	___	___	___	___
4. Creates elaborate characters or skits	___	___	___	___
5. Has a variety of vocal responses	___	___	___	___
6. Creates unique solutions	___	___	___	___
7. Can identify with moods and motives of characters	___	___	___	___
Interest, Task Commitment				
1. Participates with enthusiasm in identification activities	___	___	___	___
2. Volunteers	___	___	___	___
3. Is able to concentrate	___	___	___	___
4. Makes references to dramatic activities	___	___	___	___
5. Chooses drama-oriented activities during free time.	___	___	___	___
6. Creates plays or stories and acts in or tells them	___	___	___	___
7. Organizes others in drama activities	___	___	___	___

Please describe incidents which indicate outstanding ability, creativity, or task commitment.

compiled by Gail N. Herman

CHAPTER 8

ATTENDING TO THE GIFT

Focused attention must be given to the development of a gift or talent in its own right. Too often the strengths and interests of GLD students are either unrecognized, ignored, put on hold, or used to remediate weaknesses rather than developed or nurtured in their own right. Usually a program designed for gifted children provides this kind of nurturing. However, merely placing GLD students into an existing program for gifted students may have horrible effects. In fact, these students may not fit into existing programs for several reasons:

1. The programs may be content centered with little regard for individual strengths or interests.
2. They may place a heavy emphasis on reading and writing.
3. They may add to, instead of substitute for, existing curriculum requirements.
4. They may lack structure and guidance because it is assumed that students can produce independently.

Programs for GLD students should serve to validate individual gifts and help the students understand who they are. Specifically, the teacher must create an environment where students feel appreciated and where their gifts are both recognized and valued.

Such programs
1. Encourage students to gain information and communicate their ideas in creative ways based on individual strengths and interest.
2. Convey sophisticated content through guest speakers, demonstrations, active inquiry, visitation, films, or mentorships.
3. Use experts, equipment, and modes of inquiry of the practicing professional.
4. Acknowledge and reward individual differences of all students by offering options to all students (modification offered to a limited number of students because of a disability can give the message to bright learning-disabled students that, although a particular option is accepted, it is not preferred).

In short, programs appropriate for GLD students should have personnel who appreciate individual differences and feel comfortable highlighting student strengths. Additionally, they must minimize weaknesses in enrichment activities by helping students circumvent problematic weaknesses in pursuit of their goals. Such facilitators understand that advanced reading and writing skills are not necessarily a prerequisite for learning and creative productivity.

Essential Components

There are a variety of administrative designs available to provide opportunities to nurture the strengths and interest of GLD students. These will be described later in the chapter. First, however, it is important to elaborate further on the essential components required to assure that the needs of GLD students are met within any program. In the past, we have been involved in a number of highly successful projects purposefully designed to nurture gifts and talents in GLD students.

Although the various projects varied in design, all shared similarities which we believe were fundamental to the success of any program for GLD students. These components include the following:

1. Development of alternative modes for thinking and communicating;
2. Strategies to identify gifts in learning-disabled students;
3. Activities designed to motivate the youngsters; and
4. The use of instructional methods that highlighted the abilities of the student.

These components are described below.

Alternate Modes for Thinking and Communicating

The programs were designed to allow students to learn according to their strengths. The recent work of Howard Gardner (1983) has alerted us to the possibilities of multiple intelligences or thinking modes. He stresses that schools are organized to develop primarily linguistic talents in students. Unfortunately, many GLD students have strengths in non-verbal areas. In fact, in our work, these students were found to prefer activities in visual thinking, spatial design, and dramatic expression, as described in previous chapters. When allowed to learn in these modes, the students were highly motivated and experienced success in the programs.

Strategies to Identify Gifts

In identifying GLD students, we sought to confirm well-above-average ability in abstract thinking processes as well as documentation of specific abilities and interests. As outlined in Chapter 1, two kinds of information were collected in the identification procedure for these students: *a priori* and dynamic. *A priori* information is basically psychometric data already existing on the student from which well-above-average cognitive abilities in abstract and conceptual areas can be confirmed. An analysis of subtest scores of the Wechsler Intelligences Scale for Children-Revised (Wechsler, 1974) was particularly helpful in providing much information. We looked for scale scores of 13 and above in at least three of the following subtests: Similarities, Block Design, Comprehension, Picture Arrangement, Vocabulary, Object Assembly,

and Information. Dynamic information, on the other hand, assesses students' preferred modes of learning and communicating as well as interests. We used exploratory experiences (Renzulli's Type I) and creative activities to alert observers to the potential for students to become creative producers in specific areas. Especially important was noting creative behaviors and signs of task commitment in the children.

Motivating Activities

GLD students who have not had opportunities to use their areas of strength are accustomed to being disinterested in, and frustrated with, most learning experiences. Therefore, once these students had been selected for these programs, it was vitally important to assure them that they had been chosen to develop their special gift. Furthermore, these students were told that the goal of the experience was for them to become creative producers by having them develop products to solve real problems for real audiences (Renzulli's Type III). This information offered the students a reason for their effort. The knowledge that their work could make an impact on a real audience encouraged them to put forth effort over time to create a product of which they could be proud. The subtle, but important, message was that the students' gifts were not only recognized, but valued.

Instructional Strategies

The choice of learning mode, identification procedures, motivational techniques, and instructional strategies had to be internally consistent. For example, a child recognized for ability in dramatic expression was not asked to write down ideas before being given the opportunity to "act on them." Creative products in dramatic expression included mime, storytelling, plays and oral speaking. Likewise, visual and spatial learners were encouraged to think and create in ways unique to their mode. It was important that the selected students had an opportunity to interact with professionals who regularly used these various thinking modes to create their own products. In this way, students became the practicing professionals using methodologies, processes, and equipment that best fit how they learned.

Program Designs

Placement in Existing Programs

There are many documented cases of children doing exceptionally well in existing programs. Often, these are the students who have been recognized for their giftedness first, and their disabilities are more subtle or do not involve reading or writing. Described below are examples of typical alternatives already found in most school districts where a GLD student may attend to areas of interest in a manner suited to individual learning strengths.

Acceleration. Accelerated programs in a particular area of students strength afford the GLD student an opportunity to nurture specific talents. For instance, a student with a strong aptitude for math can find challenge in advanced courses. Here methodology, motivation, and product are aligned to the student's gift. Then the student can remain in regular or remedial classes for areas requiring a different kind of attention.

Pull-out Enrichment Programs. These programs have been proven especially successful when the student is allowed to pursue a specific interest such as computers. The opportunity to interact with peers of similar intellectual abilities and interests encourages the GLD student in developing a positive self-image. Additionally, focused attention is given to an area of strength to balance the disproportionate amount of time and energy expended on overcoming weaknesses.

Schoolwide Enrichment Model (Renzulli & Reis, 1985). Programs based on this model also have been found to be particularly effective for GLD students for several reasons. First, flexible identification allows these children to become part of the talent pool. Second, the children are offered a wide variety of activities designed to ignite student interest and encourage creative productivity. The educational experiences in this model evolve from the strengths and interests of the student in contrast to other enrichment paradigms where individual students are asked to basically conform to challenging but prescribed curriculum.

Mentorships. Another program option offered in many schools is the opportunity to take advantage of mentorships. The benefits accruing from this special relationship between mentor and mentee have been well documented. We know that learning-disabled students perform better in one-to-one settings. Added to this are unique feelings of satisfaction and self-worth gained by the student when working side by side with an expert or professional in an area of interest.

Placement in Specifically Designed Programs

Sometimes, however, it is necessary to design special programs and opportunities for GLD students. Because of learned behavior patterns, repeated failures experiences, learning and attention deficits, or the nature of the existing program, the GLD student may not fit into established programs.

In the next section, we will describe in some detail three different approaches for these students. Each program fits the general guidelines outlined earlier, but uses different administrative designs for implementation. The first describes a unique program in which handicapped gifted students are paired with mentors in areas of mutual strengths and interests.

Gifted-Handicapped Mentor Program

Putnam-Northern Westchester Board of Cooperative Services (BOCES)
Yorktown Heights, NY 10598
by Susan Levey, Coordinator

Program Goals

The major goals of the Gifted Handicapped Mentor Program (GHMP) are to enhance each student's area of giftedness and to develop a more positive self-concept. A highly skilled mentor is hired to work on a one-to-one basis with each participating student at the student's school for a minimum of one hour a week. An individualized program is developed for each student by the BOCES coordinator, working with the mentor, parent, teacher, and school.

Student Referral and Screening Procedures

A student is usually referred to the Gifted-Handicapped Mentor Program by the student's classroom teacher, special education teacher, psychologist, or by the Committee on Special Education (CSE). This is accomplished by filling out a referral form and submitting to the GHMP staff. The staff forwards the form to the student's district CSE along with a letter from BOCES requesting permission from the district to proceed with the screening. Each child referred to the GHMP has already been labeled as handicapped by the district CSE and has also demonstrated potential giftedness or specific academic aptitudes or talents.

Upon receiving permission to screen from the district, the GHMP staff starts the screening process. First, a letter goes out to the student's parents informing them of the referral and asking for their permission to screen. Program information and recent newspaper articles also are sent to the parents and they are encouraged to call with any questions they might have. Additionally, each parent is asked to return the "Permission to Screen" form. Once the "Permission to Screen" form is received, the GHMP staff then commences the screening process.

Screening for participation in the GHMP includes a thorough review of student's psychological, academic, and clinical records and interviews with the appropriate school personnel, parents and outside persons who have information to contribute to the screening process. Student interviews are conducted, classroom observation made and testing designed to determine giftedness is initiated. Because the GHMP is looking for specific academic aptitudes as well as general intellectual giftedness or specific talents, the testing and/or evaluation program is individually designed for each student.

In addition to the above screening procedures, a candidate for the GHMP in art might also be asked to submit a portfolio which is then evaluated by an artist retained by the program staff. He or she might also be given the Originality of Line Drawing Test. A writing candidate might be asked to submit samples of writing which would then be evaluated by a writer.

Other tests that might be utilized in the screening process for selected students are the *Ross Test of Higher Cognitive Thinking*, selected relevant portions of the *Scales for Rating the Behavioral Characteristics of Superior Students*, etc.

When the GHMP staff has documentation that the child has demonstrated an ability or potential ability to excel beyond the norms for children of the same age in the area of focus, the screening procedure has been completed. A screening and recommendation report is then prepared and sent to the District Committee on Special Education (CSE). If the GHMP staff and the CSE both agree on the placement and the number of hours per week recommended, the program is initiated for the student.

Individualized Student Programs

In order to initiate a student's program, a mentor must be selected. The mentor's abilities and interests must closely match those of the student and the mentor also must be motivated by a desire to share his/her skills with interested students. The mentor challenges the individual student and provides learning experiences which are appropriate to the student's ability level.

Mentor-student meetings are scheduled on a regular basis for a minimum of one hour per week during the school day. The mentor and the student must make a commitment to the program by agreeing to meet at the regularly scheduled time. Once the program is scheduled, the mentor, GHMP staff, parents, and student (if appropriate) develop an Individualized Educational Plan specifically designed to reflect the goals and objectives of the student's program. Each student is given the opportunity to accelerate or enrich learning in his/her area of particular strength.

Each mentor-student meeting is carefully planned to develop the strengths of each student by providing challenging opportunities and activities. The meetings are filled with excitement and an awareness of the potential for self-development. During the sessions, mentors establish a climate of experimentation by sharing feelings, ideas experiences, and work. The student comes to depend on the mentor for encouragement, advanced training in the area of giftedness and constructive criticism.

By attaining success in a specific area, students learn the scope and value of their abilities, skills and interests. Gaining confidence through self-discovery and achievement increases the student's satisfaction and social acceptance. The Gifted Handicapped Mentor Program, therefore, fosters individual development for the student who is both gifted and handicapped, and strengthens the total educational system.

The following describes the mentor program in action. Notice the excitement of Chris when he is allowed to create in an area of strength:

Chris, a tenth grader at Horace Greely High School in Chappaqua is learning disabled and was eligible for the Gifted-Handicapped Mentor Program.

Chris was teamed up with Paul, a sculptor, last year. This relationship was successful and extended into a summer project for the two. They met once a week for an hour and Chris learned to work in media other than clay. They worked on wood carvings and hammered metal.

"I want to swamp Chris with lots of different ideas," Paul said. "I don't want to make him a technician."

Chris agreed. "This guy is really into creativity."

The two spent five to six weeks that summer working on a bronze sculpture. The concept and design was Paul's, but the labor was shared.

"Chris did a super job," Paul said. "This was not an easy project."

From Drawings to Metal Sculpture. Paul first made several drawings and then he and Chris built a small model. They then worked out the problems on a small scale before working on the final piece. Many different processes were needed to make the sculpture. Each piece was drawn, cut out and welded. A grinding process was used to obtain a special surface. Then a patina was put on the surface.

"This was lots of fun," Chris said. "I learned a lot about metal sculpture. I like to see how an idea goes step by step, how a project on paper turns into a functional thing."

Although the sculptured piece has not yet been named, it incorporated the themes of air, wind, and birds. It will bob up and down and back and forth, giving opportunities for many different rotations. It will move with the wind and be a piece of sculpture in moving space.

Creating Chemical Climates. Paul and Chris have decided on their next project for this year—creating chemical climates in Plexiglas columns. They will construct seven-foot tall columns and use special crystals to create an ongoing ecological process which will create snow, clouds and rain.

"We're not inventing new mechanisms," Paul says. "We're using things that exist by making sculpture come alive and move in time."

According to Paul, learning sculpting techniques is only one benefit to his relationship with Chris. "The idea is to focus the mind on a goal, no matter whether it is sculpture or making banking investments. The skills he learns here can be applied to other things in his life."

For Chris, this program has been wonderful. "I've learned a lot from working with Paul. Before, I only thought about sculpting in clay. Now I think, 'How many different ways can I do this?'"

Future Plans: "Work for Myself." In high school, Chris is a goalie for the soccer team in the fall and on the track team in the spring. Although he is not sure about a future career, he is certain that he wants to be an entrepreneur and work for himself, possibly as an international art dealer. Chris will continue to work with Paul for one and a half sessions per week.

The next program was specially designed to develop the strengths and interests of GLD students. It was based on several assumptions: First that special enrichment activities must offer sophisticated challenge while circumventing problematic weaknesses and second, that the creative behavior of the students must be reinforced and valued within the school setting if it is to be maintained in a productive manner.

West Hartford Public Schools*

Project Challenge—2

Funded by Connecticut State Department of Education
The Pilot Program

Setting

Seven GLD students met every Wednesday for two and one-half hours at the District's resource center for gifted students. An important consideration in planning the program was to minimize student time lost from the regular program. The time selected for the program was an extension of a weekly shortened day used by the district for staff development purposes, thereby eliminating lost class time for students. A teacher and an intern, both specialists in gifted and special education, planned and implemented the program.

Identification

The identification process entailed screening the district's ninety-nine learning-disabled students in grades four though six for characteristics of gifted behavior.

Both test scores and teacher interviews were used to gain information about these students. Well-above-average ability was identified by assessment of scores of the Wechsler Intelligence Scale for Children-Revised (Wechsler, 1974). Students scoring at least 120 on the performance or verbal scale were selected for further screening. Fourteen students met the initial criterion. To gain information about creativity and task commitment in these students, classroom teachers and learning disabilities teachers were interviewed with an adaptation of the Scales for Rating Behavioral Characteristics of Superior Students (Renzulli *et al.*, 1977 [see Chapter 7, p.62] The adapted questionnaire consisted of twenty open-ended items from the Learning, Creativity, and Motivation subscales. The resulting information was analyzed by a team consisting of a school psychologist, a special education coordinator, and a university researcher. Each student was given a score averaged across raters based on evidence of advanced and persistent interests, creative behaviors and specific personality traits often demonstrated by creative individuals. An example of a highly rated response to the item described above is the following: "History. He reads all books on history, biography and on various periods and eras. Even though he does not read well, he spends much time absorbed in these books..." The students' final scores were derived by averaging the individual ratings. Selection for the pilot program was made by rank-ordering the fourteen students according to their average score and selecting the top seven. (Seven was determined to be an optimum number of students considering the hyperactive behavior and attention deficit problems commonly occurring in this population.)

Of the seven students identified, five were boys, two were girls; four were fourth

*   In *Gifted Child Quarterly*, Vol.32, No.1, *Winter* 1988, p.227–228. Permission to reproduce this item granted by *Gifted Child Quarterly*. The grant proposal is available from the Connecticut State Department of Education.

graders, three were fifth graders. Full scale IQ, Verbal IQ, and Performance IQ scores ranged from 134–113, 129–107, and 132–112, respectively. All students had clearly defined interests and preferred projects and experiments to written and reading assignments. Their creativity was evidenced in the clever ways they avoided tasks, their sense of humor, ideas and completed projects in science, art, and storytelling (as opposed to story writing).

The Program

The Enrichment Triad Model (Renzulli, 1977) was chosen to be used in this program. This model incorporates skill development into the production of new knowledge through the pursuit of independent or small group investigations based on the student's own interests and academic strengths. Children were encouraged to identify an area of interest and them focus on a real problem to be investigated and possibly solved. The model consists of three types of activities: general exploratory, group training, and individual and small group investigation.

General exploratory activities cover exposure to potential areas of interest and are those not necessarily found in the regular curriculum. Learning-disabled students may be introduced through lectures, demonstrations, movies, interest centers, or other approaches that bypass weaknesses in reading. These no-fail entry activities expose students to new ideas in a non-threatening atmosphere where they are given the opportunity to explore freely.

The next step—Type II Enrichment activities—provides training in such areas as critical thinking, creativity, and problem solving. Because learning-disabled children often perform better on activities using higher-level thinking skills, as opposed to simple memory and perceptual capacities (Maker, 1977), these types of activities are quite appropriate.

In Type III activities, the student becomes an investigator of a real problem—one that has not been contrived as a classroom assignment—and is guided in the development of a product that should have an authentic impact on an audience, preferably outside the school setting. The student focuses on an original idea for study and proceeds as a "practicing professional" using methods of inquiry to solve a chosen problem.

During weekly sessions, Type I and Type II experience were provided. They were designed to spark the children's interests into a future investigation and to broaden their means of effective communication to compensate for poor reading and writing skills. Specific activities included exposure to, and instruction in, photography, computer programming, and block construction.

To expose the students to the process of creative production, a student-initiated group project was undertaken. The student wrote and illustrated a unique children's book on unusual ways to pop a balloon. They designed and photographed scenes to express their ideas and wrote rhymed couplets to accompany their illustrations. To avoid using their poor handwriting, students elected to use stick-on letters, which, although tedious, was more effective in creating a professional-looking product. This project gave the students experience in staying on task, solving problems, using new communications skills and delaying gratification.

Upon completion of the book, students were encouraged to initiate individual investigations. Conferences were held with each student to assist in identifying a real problem, defining a purpose and a concerned audience for the study, and selecting a final product. A step-by-step management plan and contract with clear expectations were developed for each student to facilitate product completion. Two students designed computer programs. One program taught fifth graders about the Monitor and Merrimac; the other used random numbers to define traits of Dungeons and Dragons characters. A nine-year-old girl with limited reading and writing ability conducted a qualitative research study entitled, "A Day in the Life of Jerusha Webster" (Noah Webster's younger sister) and produced a slide and tape show which is on permanent display in the Noah Webster House. (See introduction.) Another student compared attitudes of adults and children about wearing bicycle helmets. He communicated his results on an attractive poster designed for display in bicycle shops to encourage the wearing of helmets. (See introduction.) Another young researcher prepared a dramatic slide show of fifth graders' attitudes concerning nuclear war and sent it to her state senator. Another investigation sought to create an awareness of the plight of endangered species, while another student decided to use Legos™ to create models of castles and gave a series of talks about the use of castles during the Middle Ages.

Students met with expert professionals to help them in development of the research and products. A university professor in measurement and evaluation taught several of the students to construct surveys and sample a population. Museum curators met with the students investigating historical and environmental issues. Consultants from the Lego™ Corporation offered advice to the young architect. A mentor in computers assisted the other two students in creating their computer programs. All but one project was completed and shared with the intended audience. Time needed to complete their projects ranged from four to ten weeks.

The program proved to be a huge success. Learning behaviors, self-concept, time-on-task, and task commitment showed marked improvement when the students were personally involved with their products and directed toward a goal, even when a task was tedious. Students' projects all reflected their individual learning styles, interests, and strengths. Reading and writing were abandoned in favor of hands-on experimental learning. They gained information through primary sources such as interviews, visitations, surveys and evaluation of actual artifacts. Furthermore, the students all chose to communicate their ideas through channels other than writing—slide shows, computer programs, surveys, and charts. An unexpected result was reported by parents and teachers. Academic achievement in several children improved dramatically. One student will no longer need supportive services; another gained four grade levels in reading during the year; two others have begun to show improvements in all subject areas. While there is no empirical evidence to support the contention that these academic gains can be attributed to the program, these findings do lend support to the idea that focused attention to strengths is an important, if not crucial, aspect of programs for GLD students.

The last program described here focuses again on the development of student gifts. It, unlike the others, involves a cooperative effort between the teacher of the gifted and the learning disability specialist. A particular advantage of this design was that enrichment was provided within the student's remedial program. More benefits of using this approach are discussed at the end of the description.

Rescue: Focus on Talent

funded by a grant from the
Connecticut State Department of Education

Ten districts participated in this highly successful pilot program for GLD students. The program involved a cooperative effort by the learning-disability specialist (resource-room teacher), teacher of the gifted, and mentors. The learning-disabilities specialist and the teacher of the gifted were trained to use enrichment activities to identify potential gifts in visual, spatial, or dramatic expression among their identified learning-disabled students in grades 4–8. These activities were described in Chapter 7.

Once the identification phase was completed, the teacher of the gifted and the mentors worked with groups of identified students on creative projects.

Time for enrichment in the identification stage (ten-week period) was provided by the learning-disabilities-resource-room teacher who typically saw students daily. The teachers arranged a schedule allocating four days for remediation and one day for enrichment. On the day designated for enrichment, the teacher of the gifted, together with the learning-disabilities teachers, presented the enrichment activities to the whole group of learning-disabled students. Upon completion of a set of activities, the teachers filled out structured observation checklists (see Chapter 7) as a systematic way to identify evidence of a gift or talent.

During the six- to ten-week period for this identification phase, the teachers saw a side to their students heretofore hidden. Eager, enthusiastic, and on task, all the LD students began to actually enjoy learning in such creative ways, even though a smaller number showed a specific talent or gift in particular areas.

At the end of the identification phase, teachers and mentors met to decide which of the students would be selected for phase II—working with a mentor on a group project in visual, spatial, or dramatic expression. The selected students from all districts met together with their mentors one complete day every other week over a four-month period at the regional educational center.

The students in the visual expression group used the methods of a filmmaker as they created a storyboard, wrote a script, designed costumes and scenery, figured out special effects, and filmed the final product. The students in spatial design used carpentry techniques and equipment to build a series of models demonstrating principles of applied physics.

A culminating project for this group was to design and build an intricate "Rube Goldberg" 3-D maze for the Great Marble Race. The students were required to include innovative obstacles that would impede the progress of the marble. These obstacles were to be based on the principles of physics emphasized during the enrichment sessions. The students in the dramatic expression group were transformed into professional storytellers and mimes as they gave an outstanding performance for parents and friends as a culminating activity. Two of the students actually participated in the statewide storytelling festival.

During phase II, the learning-disabilities teacher helped the individual students with assignments missed on the day they spent at the regional center. In addition, the teacher continued to use open-ended enrichment activities with other LD students to reinforce basic skills.

This particular design has several advantages:

1. Most LD children show strengths in divergent thinking experiences, especially when writing is eliminated. Thus the continued use of enrichment activities in critical and creative thinking can provide indirect reinforcement of basic skills, problem solving, and effective communication.
2. The continued use of enrichment, using inquiry and discovery in a variety of disciplines, can become a continuous search for hidden gifts and talents.
3. The team approach of using the teacher of the gifted and the LD-resource-room specialist is especially important. While learning-disability specialists can understand and relate to a child's learning problem, they have no training in enrichment strategies which can offer so much to enliven remediation. The teachers of the gifted can model these activities with the group, and, in doing so, broaden their own perspective of who may be gifted. Teachers of the gifted very often marvel at the creative abilities of learning-disabled children.
4. The use of both teachers as resources is vitally important when a gift is identified. Because teachers of the gifted are well-versed in developing gifts, it makes the most sense that they assume the responsibility for more advanced enrichment. On the other hand, the LD teacher is in the best position to provide academic support for work missed when students are completing creative products.

The possibilities available to nurture the strengths and interests of GLD students are endless. However, educators first need to be convinced of the need to focus attention on the gifts of these students,. Second, they must make a financial commitment to serve this population appropriately.

CHAPTER 9

INSTRUCTIONAL STRATEGIES

Perhaps the most important challenge educators face in providing appropriate programs for GLD students is maximizing student success while minimizing failure and frustration. In arranging successful learning experiences, it is useful to consider the major factors contributing to the GLD's lack of success: the learning disability itself, the student's negative attitudes about self and school, and poor motivation for school-related tasks. Children diagnosed as learning disabled often have difficulties in one or more of the following areas, making high achievement difficult:

1. Acquiring information, especially from print materials;
2. Organizing information and tasks;
3. Remembering isolated information and facts;
4. Communicating ideas, especially in writing.

Thus, these bright students are faced with the frustration of learning in ways that highlight their disability. Coupled with on-going failure at accomplishing simple tasks such as memorizing math facts or spelling words, these students begin to question their ability as learners.

Remedial efforts by definition highlight weaknesses and emphasize the simplest of tasks, for which a bright child usually shows negative enthusiasm. As a result, GLD students begin to regard school as irrelevant. They may generalize feelings about specific areas of weakness to a general feeling of depression or hostility. Not only do they develop negative feelings about their abilities, but they develop negative feelings about their worth as students and human beings as well.

Where to Begin

We have found that the best starting point to help GLD students reverse poor motivation patterns, negative attitudes and failure experiences is to have them feel the exhilaration of achieving a goal that is important to them. In this kind of experience, success is defined as performance that meets the internal standards of the students on tasks deemed important and relevant. It is precisely for this reason that we have emphasized approaches typically encouraged for gifted students. A curriculum that respects intelligence and offers sophisticated challenge and personal relevance will afford GLD students the opportunity to achieve high quality success.

Suggestions for teacher strategies that address these issues and have been helpful in enabling GLD students to achieve success are described below. These strategies fall into four categories; 1) selecting appropriate activities, 2) helping students compensate for weaknesses, 3) managing behavior, and 4) offering emotional support. These strategies should be applied to both enrichment activities and to the regular curriculum.

Selecting Appropriate Activities

As a rule, activities or experiences provided for a GLD student should be purposeful, interesting, and respect the intellectual ability of the student. Creating interest, a desire to know, or setting a meaningful goal to be reached will make the hard effort required by the child a worthwhile undertaking.

The following guidelines should help educators plan meaningful experiences:

1. Use activities that require active inquiry involving discussion and experimentation. Because these children have difficulty reading and remembering, learning experiences that are more inviting and interactive are especially suitable for them to gain information and process it. Using strategies in which students are actively involved in their learning will enhance their ability to acquire information and remember. GLD students have no difficulty attending to task and paying attention when offered exciting activities that require them to act, do, discuss or experiment.

2. Provide open-ended challenges that require divergent thinking, especially in small group settings. According to research, gifted, learning-disabled children have considerable strength in creative thinking. Where more unusual answers are preferred, these students can excel. Such opportunities will enhance their self-esteem. Also experiences that will improve their divergent thinking ability will empower these students to create alternate ways to reach goals and solve problems that avoid their learning problems. Programs such as *Creative Problem Solving, Synectics,* and *Talents Unlimited* are especially suited to the learning abilities of GLD students. These programs offer a systematic approach that requires critical and creative thinking to solve problems and produce high quality responses. The techniques are easily applied to both enrichment activities and the regular curriculum. The resources listed below offer detailed information on these teaching approaches and activities to use with your students.

3. Offer options that enable students to use their strengths and preferred learning styles. As discussed earlier, using drama, film making and spatial design activities, for instance, will allow the gift as well as acquired knowledge to be expressed. In fact, these students will be much more willing to put forth concentrated effort, and consequently, the quality of the finished product will improve greatly.

4. Set aside time for the students to pursue areas of interests using the methods and materials of the

---

Creative Problem Solving

Noller, R., Parnes, S., & Biondi A. *Creative Action Book.* NY: Charles Scribner's Sons

The following are available through D.O.K. Publishers, P.O. Box 605, East Aurora, New York 14052:

Eberle, B., & Stanish, B. *CPS for Kids: A Resource Book for Teaching Creative Problem-Solving to Children.* For Grades 3–9

Noller, R.B., Heintz, R.E., Blaeuer, D.A., & Mauthe, E. *Creative Problem-Solving in Mathematics.*

Stanish, B. & Eberls, B. *Be a Problem-Solver.* For Grades 4–12

Flack, J.D. *Once Upon a Time (CPS Through Fairy Tales).*

Duling, G.A. *Creative Problem-Solving for an Eency Weency Spider.*

Synectics

Gordon, W., & Poze, T. *Strange & Familiar Series.* SES Associates
121 Brattle Street, Cambridge, MA 02138

Talents Unlimited

Dr. Carol Schlicter, University of Alabama, College of Ed., P.O. Box 2592, Tuscaloosa, AL 35487

practicing professional. According to Maslow (1968), each of us is driven naturally to self-actualize, or become what we can be in areas of passion and strength. The use of professional methodologies and equipment permits the GLD students to know that individual gifts are valued and respected. More importantly, it reinforces their belief that creative productivity is a realistic objective.

Many how-to books detail the real world methods used by the practicing professional to create new knowledge or products. An excellent resource for teachers is the Methodological Resources section of the catalog distributed by Creative Learning Press. Books listed in the catalog provide youngsters with the knowledge of how to be a photographer, scientist or entrepreneur. It is this sort of learning-by-doing experiences that the GLD student finds challenging and rewarding.

5. When possible, incorporate opportunities for students to investigate real problems for real audiences in areas of interest. In our work, GLD students made the most gains when involved in such activities. For more detail, see *The Enrichment Triad Model: A Guide for Developing Defensible Programs for Gifted and Talented* (Renzulli, 1977).

Compensation Strategies

The learning problems connected with a learning disability tend to be somewhat permanent through life. A poor speller always will have to check for spelling errors (or rely on a computer spell checker) before submitting a final draft. Students who have difficulty memorizing math facts might need to assure accuracy by using a calculator. Thus, to simply remediate weaknesses may not be appropriate for the GLD child. Remediation may make the learner somewhat more proficient, but probably not excellent, in areas of weakness. We must seriously consider when to use compensation techniques in favor of remedial strategies. For example, we should ask, "To what extent do we help children to improve handwriting before encouraging them to put their thoughts on paper using a word processor?"

At this point it is important to remember the distinction between a disability and a handicap.

> Disabilities are physical states or conditions that result in impairment of functioning...Disabilities become handicaps when they interfere with the individual's ability to function in specific situations. (Lewis & Doorlag, 1983, p.50)

Learning-disabled children have been found to be intelligent and productive outside the school environment. They learn, create, and perform well. In school, however, they become handicapped—required to do tasks that are extremely difficult because of a neurological or information processing disorder. In helping the child to achieve success in school, we should determine whether the environment is creating the handicap.

Consider the student who has an excellent understanding of mathematical concepts but has great difficulty remembering math facts. What will be in the student's best interest—to give him thirty minutes a day of drill or to allow the student to use a calculator? Will a small adjustment to the environment prevent the disability from becoming a handicap? Perhaps the use of the calculator on drill exercises will enable the youngster to remember the facts as well.

In this section of the chapter, we will discuss some compensation strategies useful in helping GLD students to overcome their learning difficulties. Table 9.1 summarizes some of the major difficulties GLD students experience in school and some practical tips for helping the students to compensate for them. These ideas are explained more fully in the next several pages.

Ways for GLD Students with Limited Reading Skills to Acquire Information

It is important for bright students who have problems with decoding written information to have information-gathering options that do not insult their intelligence. Using inquiry methods and primary sources are exciting and sophisticated ways of learning. Field trips related to the topics in the required curriculum can provide these students with a great deal of content. Using visual aids such as films, television documentaries, live drama, and computer software packages are especially useful in conveying facts and new information to the student. Lectures, taped interviews and tapes of books also provide relevant data.

A particularly effective source for the student who is a visual learner is picture books. Picture books today exist for all age groups on a wide range of topics. High quality illustrations offer a wealth of content which provides a context from which the student can probably read and comprehend the test. History buffs, for example, can spend days pouring over the visual accounts of the battles of the Civil War. The pictures offer invitations for inquiry and further pursuit. Original selections from Emily Dickinson, Shakespeare, Browning, and Frost are some of the literary figures explored in picture books. These books can be used with youngsters from four to forty. Listed on page 94 are some choice titles you may consider. They are arranged by disciplines and can be used as an introduction into a field of study.

Another area where GLD students have trouble is completing assignments on worksheet pages. They may become overwhelmed by the amount of information on the page and not be able to understand the written directions or content contained on the page. Teaching materials that we use with these students should be selected with care. These materials should have limited content on a page and be inquiry based if possible. But most importantly, there should be a visual component that can supply content necessary to complete the learning objective. Today there are many teacher resources that use critical and creative thinking activities to reinforce basic skills and enrich the regular curriculum.

Consider the following sample activities. The first (Picnic) is a novel approach to teaching reading comprehension skills by having the students solve a mystery (inquiry based). Many of the necessary details are provided in the picture (visual component) and the instructions for solving the puzzle are direct and to the point (limited content on a page). Because the activity presents a strategy for solving the problem, the GLD student may be shown that strategy can be applied to other situations (see Chapter 6).

Table 9.1 Common Learning Problems of GLD Students and Corresponding Compensation Tips

Problem	*Compensation Tip*
Acquiring information with limited reading skills	Use nonprint experiences Use picture books Use teaching materials that have a visual component
Organizing information	Use advanced organizers, visual models and recipes Use worksheets with a response format Teach strategies for organizing: webbing, storyboards, Venn Diagrams and matrices
Remembering details and assignments	Use mnemonic devices Use visual imagery Establish a buddy system
Demonstrating poor skills in handwriting and spelling	Use computer word processing programs
Feeling valued	Provide opportunities for cooperative learning where *each* member contributes his strength

Picture Book Bibliography

Biology

Heller, R. (1981) *Chickens aren't the only ones.* New York: G.P. Putnam's Sons.

Heller, R. (1982) *Animals born alive and well.* New York: Grossett and Dunlap.

Lear, E. with Nash, O. (1968) *Scroobious pip.* NY: Harper & Row Publishers.

McCord, A. (1977) *Dinosaurs.* Tulsa, OK: EDC Publishing Co.

Pienkowski, J. (1980) *Dinner time.* Los Angeles: Price, Stern, Sloan Publishers, Inc.

Stout, W., Service, W. & Preiss, B. (1981) *The Dinosaurs.* New York: Bantam Books.

Geology

McClerran, A. (1985) *The mountain who loved a bird.* Natick, MA: Picture Book Studio USA.

Siebert, D. (1988) *Mojave.* New York: Thomas Y. Crowell.

Botany

Butcher, J. (1984) *The sheep and the rowan tree.* New York: Holt, Rinehart, & Winston

Heller, R. (1983) *The reason for a flower.* New York: Grossett

Mathematics

Anno, M. (1985) *Anno's hat trick.* New York: Philomel Books.

Anno, M. (1986) *All in a day.* New York: Philomel Books.

Anno, M. (1986) *Socrates and the three little pigs.* New York: Philomel Books.

Korab, B. (1985) *Archabet.* Washington, DC: The Preservation Press.

Psychology (Social and Emotional Issues)

de Paola, T. (1983) *Sing Pierot sing.* New York: Harcourt, Brace, and Jovanovich.

Espeland, P., & Waniak M. (1980) *The cat walked through the casserole.* Minneapolis: Carolahoda Books, Inc.

Locker, T. (1985) *The mare on the hill.* New York: Dial Books.

Martin, B. & Archambault, J. (1987) *Knots on a counting rope.* New York: Henry Holt & Co.

Pienkowski, J. (1983) *Small Talk.* Los Angeles: Price, Stern, Sloan Publishers, Inc.

Steiner, T. (1976) *The warm fuzzy tale.* Sacramento, CA: Jalmar Press.

Walker, A. (1988) *To hell with dying.* NY: Harcourt, Brace, Jovanovich

Literature/Writing

Browning, R. with Ianov, A. (1986) *The pied piper of Hamlin.* New York, Lothrop, Lee, & Shepard.

Dickinson, E. (1978) *I'm nobody! Who are you?* Owings Mills, Maryland: Stemmer House.

Eliot, T.S. with LeCain, E. (1986) *Growtiger's last stand and other poems.* New York: Harcourt, Brace & Jovanovich.

Frost, R. with Jeffers, S. (1978) *Stopping by woods on a snowy evening.* New York: Dutton.

Heller, R. (1987) *A cache of jewels and other collective nouns.* New York: Grosset & Dunlap.

Longfellow, W. with Jeffers. S. (1983) *Hiawatha.* New York: Dial Books.

Shakespeare, W. (1980) *Under the greenwood tree.* Owings Mills, Maryland: Stemmer House.

Van Allsburg, C. (1984) *The mysteries of Harris Burlick.* Boston: Houghton Mifflin.

Wood, A. (1982) *Quick as a cricket.* Singapore: Child's Play International Ltd.

Anthropology

Aardema, V. (1981) *Bringing the rain to Kapiti.* New York: Dial Books.

Anno, M. (1981) *Anno's Britain.* New York: Philomel Books.

Cox, D. (1983) *Ayu and the Perfect Moon.* Toronto: The Bodley Head.

de Paola, T. (1983) *The legend of the bluebonnet.* New York: G.P. Putnam's Sons.

Musgrove, M. (1976) *Ashanti to Zulu.* New York: Dial Books.

Sociology

MacCauley, D. (1985) *Baa.* Boston: Houghton Mifflin Co.

Provenson, A. & Provenson, M. (1987) *Shaker Lane,* New York: Viking Penguin Inc.

History

Aliki. (1983) *A Medieval feast.* New York: Thomas Y. Crowell.

Gerrard, R. (1988) *Sir Francis Drake: His daring deeds.* New York: Farrar Straus Giroux.

Goodall, J. (1986) *The story of a castle.* New York: Margaret K. McElderry Books, Macmillan Publishing Co.

Goodall, J. (1987) *The story of a Main Street.* New York: Margaret K. McElderry, Macmillan Publishing Co.

Hartley, D. (1986) *Up north in winter.* New York: E.P. Dutton.

Hendershot, J. (1987) *In coal country.* New York: Alfred A. Knopf.

Levinson, R. (1985) *Watch the stars come out.* New York: E.F. Dutton.

Provenson, A. & Provenson, M. (1984) *Leonardo Da Vinci.* New York: The Viking Press.

Seawall, M. (1986) *The Pilgrims of Plimoth.* New York: Atheneum.

Wellman, O. & Hotze, B. (1982) *Grandpa's story.* Hermann, MO: The Hot Z Co.

Winter, J. (1988) *Follow the drinking gourd.* New York: Alfred A. Knopf.

Fine Arts or Aesthetics

Clement, C. & Clement, F. (1986) *The painter and the wild swans.* New York: Dial Books.

Clement, C. & Clement, F. (1989) *The voice of the wood.* New York: Dial Books.

Fleischman, P. (1988) *Rondo in C.* New York: Harper and Row.

Raboff, E. (1979) *Paul Klee.* (Art Start Books) New York: Doubleday & Co., Inc.

Striker, S. (1980) *The great masterpieces—Anti-coloring book.* New York: Holt Rinehart & Winston.

PICNIC

You're the Detective*

Every morning the Fancy family chauffeur brought Gwendolyn to school, and every evening he called for her in one of the Fancy limousines (usually the red one), and every week she wore a new dress (usually a red one). She showed it off and told her classmates how rich she was.

When the class decided to have a picnic on Dead Pirate's Beach, and to swim and roast marshmallows, Gwendolyn surprised everybody by saying that she'd love to go. The chauffeur brought her to the beach and immediately took a shine to the teacher. Meanwhile, Gwendolyn told her classmates that it was her birthday and that she'd been given a watch worth a thousand dollars. She showed it off and made everybody admire it, and she kept saying how expensive it was.

Gwendolyn went for a swim with the others, but when she returned to the beach her watch was gone. She cried and cried and said she *knew* that she'd put the watch down carefully with her possessions before she went in the water. The chauffeur called the police, who searched everywhere

* From *You're the Detective*, page 20 by L. Treat. Copyright © 1983 by Lawrence Treat. Reprinted by permission of David Godine, Publisher.

and talked to everybody, but couldn't find the watch. Nevertheless, Whiz McGonnigle, who , like everybody else, had no love for Gwendolyn, was pretty sure he could have found the watch, but he kept mum.

Where do you think he would have looked?

Questions

1. Are Gwendolyn's things the ones with the picnic basket and other beach items?
   Yes_____ No_____

2. Are expensive watches usually thin? Yes_____ No_____

3. Is a thin watch easy to conceal? Yes_____ No_____

4. Would the watch gleam in the sunlight? Yes_____ No_____

5. Do you think someone took the watch without being seen? Yes_____ No_____

6. Do you think that Gwendolyn lost the watch in the water, and then made up the theft story?
   Yes_____ No_____

7. Where do you think Whiz thought he could have found the watch?

Answers

1. Yes, judging by the expensive clothes and beach equipment.

2. Yes. That's one of the characteristics that marks them as expensive.

3. Yes

4. Yes

5. No. The teacher and the chauffeur are near Gwendolyn's things and would surely have noticed anyone meddling.

6. No. She was too fond of her new watch to have taken it into the water.

7. Crows are notorious for being attracted by shiny objects, and it is highly likely that a crow picked up the watch and flew off with it. The likelihood is increased by the presence of the crows, of bird tracks near Gwendolyn's clothes, and of a crow's nest in the tree.

The second activity is taken from a learning kit called *Photo Search* published by Learning Seed. It uses intriguing photographs from different events in history to challenge students to become historians by uncovering the events shown in the pictures. This is an exciting method for teaching the research skills of hypothesizing, collecting supportive data, and drawing conclusions. All of these skills can be generalized to other areas of the curriculum.

The caption to the picture on the following page is "Members of the Mochida family awaiting evacuation bus." Explain what is happening and when this picture was taken.

Answer: The family is awaiting an evacuation bus to take them to one of the detention camps set up for Japanese living in the United States during World War II. The picture was taken May 8, 1942. Researchers should be able to report on the camps and the reasons for their existence.

Strategies for Improving Poor Organizational Skills

Gifted, learning-disabled students often have difficulty organizing information sequentially. This problem can affect their ability to receive, process, and communicate information as we discussed in Chapter 5. For example, when they try to take notes during a lecture, they can become confused as to how to organize the content into major topics and subtopics. Each fact can appear to be a separate and equal entity, putting a sizable strain on their capacity to remember. Manipulating ideas in their head can also be difficult. In that case, they succeed much better when they can see the possibilities in front of them. Likewise, when they are asked to write a report or create a display of some kind, a visual model may provide an organizational cue that will assure success. Following are some specific things that you can do to help GLD students with organization in receiving, processing, and communicating information.

It is helpful for GLD students to see the bigger picture before they are given details. One way to accomplish this is to provide the students with advance outlines of a lecture with spaces to fill in details. In addition, if you project an overhead transparency of this outline and use it to indicate to your students where you are in your presentation, the students will have an easier time following the pattern of the lesson. Also, presenting a brief overview of the lesson's *purpose* and how you plan to cover the information will give the GLD student the bigger picture. This picture will become the structure needed to organize the content. A popular suggestion for teachers has been to allow the LD student who has difficulty writing to tape lectures. If, in addition, this same student has difficulty with organization, the outline will be needed as well.

Another way to give students the bigger picture is to inform their parents of the topics you will be covering during the year. This will allow the families the opportunity to arrange family outings to a museum, play or historic site related to the curriculum. In this way, the GLD student will have rich memories to which he can link new information covered in class.

A simple but beneficial approach is to make an adjustment in the order that work is assigned. The usual sequence when teaching a unit is to assign readings or provide content first, then test the students on the content. When we are assured of mastery, we may assign as interesting project to enrich the unit. With GLD students, a more motivating approach is to challenge them first with a creative project relating to the topic. Their reading and research are directed toward a specific goal that is more meaningful than doing well on a test. For example, if the student has a talent in drawing, his project might be a mural depicting the life of the Navajo Indians during the 1800's. The content needed to complete the project will steer the student's attention and activity in the learning process. His learning of the content will improve. What information is provided through his own project and the projects of the other students will probably have a positive influence on mastery of unit objectives.

Because GLD students are often holistic thinkers, their ideas do not emerge in an orderly form. Planning a project or a piece of writing can be a formidable task because these students simply do not know where to begin. The use of webbing or mapping can be a life saver to these students. Webbing allows the student to get seemingly random and disconnected ideas down on paper where lines can be drawn connecting these thoughts. The main topic or idea is centered on the paper, and the student lists ideas related to the topic. Once the ideas are down on paper, the student can begin to categorize the pieces into subtopics. New and more focused webs can then be generated and details added as needed. The visual picture of the aspects related to the topic readily evolves into an outline. The major subtopics become the Roman Numerals, and the details listed under those headings become the letters of the outline.

Pictured on the next page is a web used to help Debra, the young historian, (Chapters 1 and 6) to generate ideas and organize her research on Jerusha Webster. This web was used to discuss some ideas that were fuzzy. Debra had shown a talent in photography and historical research. She had expressed a desire to conduct a study about a family portrayed in an antique album used by her teacher to introduce the class to historical inquiry. Because such a venture was impossible, the teacher explored other possibilities with her. The web was a "picture" of the discussion.

After generating some tentative ideas, Debra explored some of the possibilities to see which one

Web 1

General Topic   **"Fuzzy Problem"**

"I like historical research and I would like to include photography."

Picture Book
History of Capitol Building

Photographic Essay
History of a Building

Slide Show

Photography

Historical Research

People from
West Hartford
1. Noah Webster
2.

History of Building
1. Old Statehouse.
2. Mark Twain House
3. Harriet Beecher Stow House
4. Capitol

Eras
1. Colonial
2. Civil War
3. 1900's

---

was most appealing and feasible. The initial investigation included a trip to the Noah Webster House. Debra was enchanted with the artifacts and historical lore all around her. The curator, sensing her excitement, asked Debra if she would be interested in contributing to the collection. He suggested that Debra create a slide and tape show about what it was like to live during colonial times through the eyes of Jerusha Webster, Noah Webster's sister. Debra leaped at the opportunity. She then needed a second web to help her plan her research. After carefully considering possible topics to be included, the next web was developed. (See page 100.) This format led to some research questions, an outline, and potential resources for finding information.

Listed below are three excellent sources for webbing techniques:

Heimlich, J.E. & Pittleman, S.D. (1986). *Semantic mapping: Classroom applications.* Newark, DE: International Reading Association.
Large, C. (1987). *The clustering approach to better essay writing.* Monroe, NY: Trillium Press.
Rico, G.L. (1983). *Writing the natural way.* Los Angeles: J.P. Tarcher.

Another strategy for organizing a project or story is the use of storyboarding. A pictorial sketch with details added can help gifted-LD students sequence the events in a story, create a mood, and elaborate on an idea as filmmakers do. The use of storyboarding was described in Chapter 7 and resources provided. Drawing a storyboard can additionally help the GLD student remember the order of things. Consider the storyboard pictured on the next page which sketches out some of the events leading up to the American Revolution. The student need not be an artist; stick figures and words here and there will suffice. Again, any technique in which the student actively interacts with the content to see the information can enhance the student's learning.

Web 2

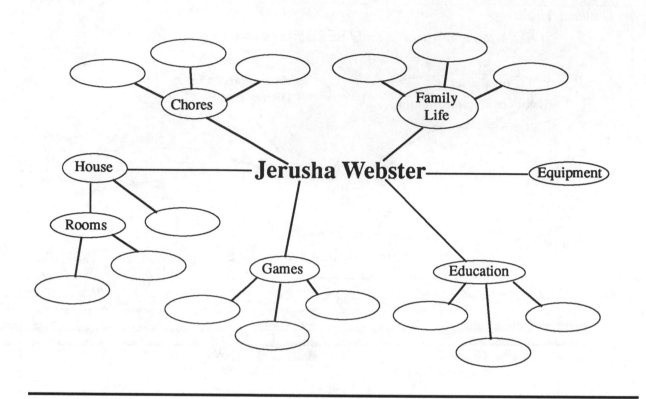

Storyboard

Events leading up to the Revolution

Formats or recipes for research papers or displays are other organizers to help the GLD student to put ideas in writing. The outline on the next page was developed to help students write speeches. We have found that it serves as a recipe for writing as well.

Likewise, this sketch of a display board for a science fair project will provide the student with a visual model or standard of what his final product should look like.

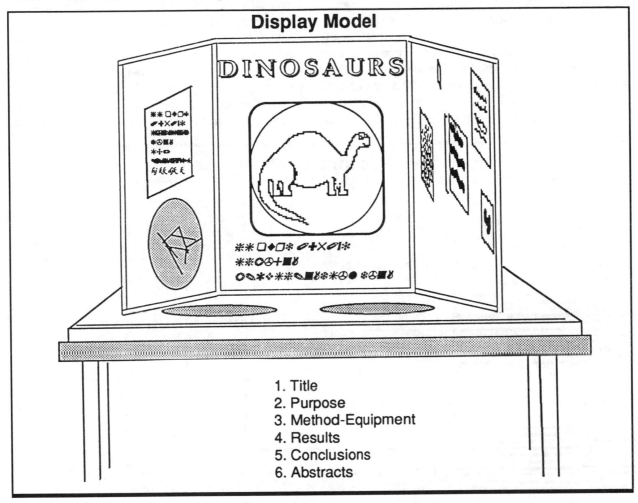

Display Model

DINOSAURS

1. Title
2. Purpose
3. Method-Equipment
4. Results
5. Conclusions
6. Abstracts

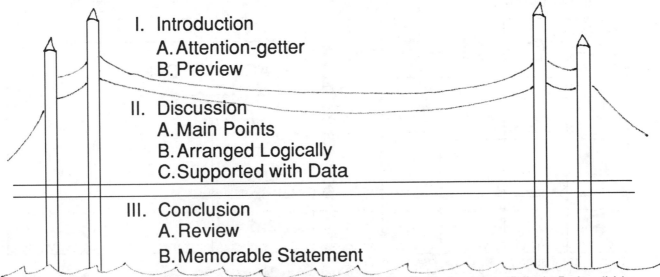

Speech Format

I. Introduction
   A. Attention-getter
   B. Preview

II. Discussion
   A. Main Points
   B. Arranged Logically
   C. Supported with Data

III. Conclusion
   A. Review
   B. Memorable Statement

Many GLD students have difficulty organizing responses on simple assignments and worksheets. Their answers do not seem to be in any recognizable order, which causes great difficulty in grading the work. To assist them in completing work that is neatly organized, students should be provided with structured response sheets. These sheets address two vital issues. First, they enable GLD students to complete work that is neat and easier to read. Second, these materials provide a visual model for organization. A discussion of how the sheet is set up so that information is clear and easily understood will allow these students to incorporate the strategy into their own repertoire.

It is important to select materials that both stimulate the students' thinking and provide them with a way to organize their responses. Notice the two activity sheets shown below. They not only offer interesting challenges but provide the students with a structure for recording their answers.

Deductive Reasoning—Transitive Order

F-168 A mouse, a rabbit, and a tiger are called Cicero, Ego, or Fred.
From the clues below, match the name with the animal.

a. Ego is larger than a mouse.
b. Cicero is older than the rabbit, but younger than the tiger.
c. Fred is older than Cicero

	M	R	T
C			
E			
F			

F-169 Three racing car drivers named Graham, Mario, and Pancho entered cars in a 24-hour race and each won a prize. From the following clues, determine who drove each car and what prize was won by each driver.

a. The coupe won a higher prize than Mario's car.
b. Mario did not drive the Spyder
c. A hatchback won the prize.
d. Graham's car won first place.
e. The Spyder came in second.

	C	H	S
G			
M			
P			

PLACE	CAR	DRIVER
1st		
2nd		
3rd		

From *Building Thinking Skills—Book 2*, page 207. Reprinted with permission of Midwest Publications.

Rolling a Die

This is a die.
Two of them are called dice.

When you play COOTIE, you roll one die.
When you play MONOPOLY, you roll two dice.
When you play YAHTZEE, you roll five dice.

A die may show any of these on its top face:

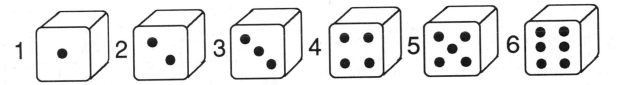

Roll a die 60 times. Keep a tally of how many 1's, 2's, 3's, 4's, 5's and 6's you get.

Number of dots	Tally	Number
1		
2		
3		
4		
5		
6		
Total		

Do the results surprise you?_____

Why or why not?_____

The next examples are work sheets designed by teachers for teacher-made activities. The first was an activity sheet purposefully designed to structure a trip to a museum. The second was used with GLD students in a hands-on evaluation activity. Notice how both sheets provide an organizational structure that informs students what is required and how it is to be recorded.

Lutz Children's Museum Scavenger Hunt

1. **TAKE A SURVEY**
   a. How many animals do you see?_____
   b. Keep a tally of how many animals are herbivorous, carnivorous, omnivorous:

	Mammals	Birds	Reptiles
Herbivorous			
Carnivorous			
Omnivorous			

2. **TOY DEMONSTRATION**
   Pretend you live in the year 1900. What three toys would you choose?

   1. _____

   2. _____

   3. _____

3. **QUILT**
   a. How many layers in a quilt?_____
   b. Draw your favorite pattern from those you see *or* design your own.

4. **PUPPET THEATRE**
   Here is your challenge:
   a. With a partner, design a one-minute skit. You may use rod puppets, hand puppets, or pretend you are a puppet.
   b. You will have ten (10) minutes of planning time.
   c. Remember, you only have one (1) minute.

5. **ALBERT SCHWEITZER EXHIBIT**
   Which team can find the most clues about the life of Albert Schweitzer?

   1._____ 2._____

   3._____ 4._____

   5._____ 6._____

   7._____ 8._____

Evaluation Exercise:
The Most Practical Way to Break a Balloon

	Total	Ease of getting materials	Time; Speed	# of Trial	Low Cost
Shaving the Balloon	12	3	3	4 6 3	3
Smash with Dictionary	6	1	1	1	3
Stick with Pin	4	1	5 6 5 1	1	1
Hold over heat	5	1	1	1	2

Rating: 1-excellent; 2-average; 3-poor   3

As we discussed before, GLD students often have difficulty mentally manipulating ideas to process information systematically. Webbing or mapping was one idea we suggested to allow students to view their ideas as they categorized and sequenced them. There are other visual techniques that GLD students can use to help them organize their thinking. One strategy is using Venn diagrams when asked to compare and contrast particular topics. These diagrams also offer students a picture of how classes of information are related to each other. Once a picture of relationships can be established, it becomes an easy task to describe it. Midwest Publications offers many materials to teach students how to use Venn diagrams. Four such activities are pictured on the following page. These thinking skills activities are excellent in teaching the students to understand the strategy. However, it is up to the teacher to help the student to apply the technique to curricular areas.

The last strategy we will discuss for helping students organize their thinking and communicating is the use of flow charts. Like Venn Diagrams, they offer students a means of organizing information visually in order to get a clear picture of relationships among facts and concepts. Shown on page 107 is a sample activity of designed practice using flow charts.

Ideas for Enhancing Memory Skills in GLD Students

As we noted in Chapter 5, problems in memory are a major characteristics of GLD students. Problems in remembering facts and details in isolation present tall hurdles for these students. As a result, many are poor spellers, forget phone numbers, and never get those math facts mastered. One way to help these students with problems in memory is to teach how to invent mnemonics or funny ways to remember the little details so easily lost. We have all used this device to remember that the principal is your pal, or that Roy G. Biv stands for the colors of the spectrum. The strategy works best when the student thinks up an original mnemonic.

Another strategy is to use visual imagery to help encode details into a meaningful context. For example, if you are teaching the water cycle in science, you might have your students close their eyes and picture Ronnie Raindrop as he begins his trip. Have them feel the rain and listen to its patter. Ask them what Ronnie might be saying as he tumbles to the earth. Have them hear the splash as he lands in the puddle. Ask them to tell you what he is thinking as he rests in the muddy puddle. Have them feel the sun peeping out behind the cloud as it spreads its warmth to the ground below. Describe

Diagramming Classes

Diagrams can be used to show relationships.

EXAMPLE: bicycles, trucks, vehicles
The first diagram pictures two distinctly different classes within a common class. The large circle represents vehicles. The smaller circles represent bicycles and trucks.
A bicycle is a kind of vehicle and a truck is a kind of vehicle. However, no truck is a bicycle.

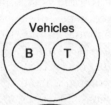

EXAMPLE: truck, van, vehicle
The second diagram pictures a class-subclass relationship. All of the items in one class are members of a larger class.
A truck is a kind of vehicle, and a van is a kind of truck. The smaller circle representing trucks is inside the large circle representing vehicles because all trucks are vehicles. The smallest circle representing vans is inside the circle representing trucks because all vans are trucks.

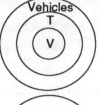

EXAMPLE: bicycles, mopeds, motorcycles, vehicles
Is there a form of bicycle that is also a form of motorcycle?
A moped can be operated by peddling like a bicycle. A moped can also be powered by its engine like a motorcycle. This relationship can be shown by an overlapping diagram like this one:

V = vans, B = bicycles, C = motorcycles, M = mopeds

Diagramming Classes—Select

Select the diagram that pictures the way in which the words can be correctly classified. Put an "X" through the diagram which cannot be used for this group of words. Label the parts of the correct diagram to show the word relationship.

G–119   Word group: coins (c),
coins for collecting (cc),
coins for spending (cs).

G–120   Word group: coins (c),
dimes (d),
money (m).

Diagramming Classes—Select

Draw a line from the group of words to the diagram which pictures the correct relationship. Use the abbreviations in the parentheses to label the diagrams correctly.

WORD GROUPS	DIAGRAMS	WORD GROUPS	DIAGRAMS
G–121 Food (Fo) Food that grows on vines (Fv) Fruit (fr)		**G–124** Birds (B) Chickens (C) Ducks (D)	
G–122 Food (Fo) Fruit (Fr) Oranges (O)		**G–125** Birds (B) Ducks (D) Wild Birds (WB)	
G–123 Food (Fo) Fruit (Fr) Vegetables (V)		**G–126** Birds (B) Chickens (C) Hens (H)	

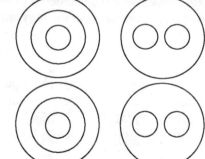

From *Building Thinking Skills—Book 2*, page2 252–255. Reprinted with permission of Midwest Publications.

how Ronnie is soaking up the sun, feeling warm and content. All of a sudden he feels as light as air. As a matter of fact, Ronnie has evaporated into the air and is swirling up towards the clouds where he rests comfortably. Have them imagine other evaporated water droplets joining with Ronnie. Tell the students to picture all the raindrops holding hands together dancing and playing until there are so many that they form a cloud. Ronnie moans that things are getting crowded and he feels bloated and damp. He is getting so heavy. Watch! He's falling, falling. Listen! Hear him call out, "Here I go again!" Guided images like this help the students put facts into a story or scene that they can conjure up when asked to recall details. There are a variety of resources available for using visualization techniques with your students. Following are several choices.

Bagley, M. & Hess, K. (1984). *Two hundred ways of using imagery in the classroom.* Monroe, NY: Trillium Press

Bagley, M. (1985). *Using imagery in creative problem solving.* Monroe, NY: Trillium Press.

Bagley. M. (1988). *Using Imagery to develop memory.* Monroe, NY: Trillium Press.

Hess, K. (1986). *Enhancing writing through imagery.* Monroe, NY: Trillium Press.

Students themselves report that what they remember best is information gained from a lively discussion, an experiment they conduct or a simulation in which they have participated. In other words, the more active the learning activity is, the more likely information from it will be captured in long-term memory.

Using Technology to Circumvent Poor Skills in Writing and Spelling

Technology has become vitally important in enabling GLD students to reach high levels of achievement. Through the use of technology, the GLD student is able to access and organize information, increase accuracy in mathematics and spelling, and improve the visual quality of the finished product. In short, when GLD students

Thinking Skills: Verbal Classifications

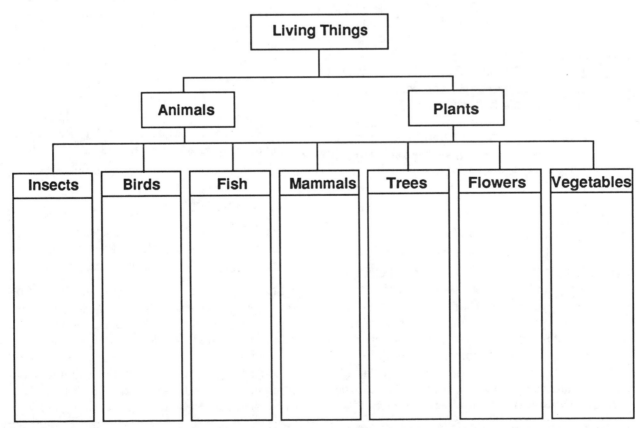

From *Building Thinking Skills—Book 2*, page 251. Reprinted with permission of Midwest Publications.

complete assignments on the computer, they can rapidly produce work that will make them proud…and surprise most observers. When these students are denied access to technology, their disability begins to look like a real handicap.

In a world with unlimited resources, every GLD student would complete written assignments on a computer. The students who have been fortunate enough to have had this opportunity have shown remarkable improvement in their writing. They report a sudden sense of empowerment, as though an evil curse has been lifted. Not only does the finished product look neater, but these students have a much easier time reading and revising drafts. Another benefit is that phonetic spelling is recognized by many dictionary programs and enables the poor speller to correct errors. This fact alone is reason to teach GLD students to spell phonetically, especially when students strong in Integrative Intelligence prefer this approach. It is also apparent that using a computer eliminates a step for those students who have not developed automaticity in writing. No longer do they have to think about how to form letters while trying to keep a complex idea in mind; instead they simply touch a key. (Two-finger typing is as acceptable as keyboard mastery.) One student we know who had horrible handwriting began doing his homework on the computer. Now he is more willing to sit down to do his written assignments; and he put substantially more time and effort into his work. He composed more effective sentences and better organized paragraphs. His restless behavior was nearly evaporated. His teacher, too, appreciated the improvement in his work and commented to him, "God will bless you for getting a computer and printer!"

Considerations Which Enable GLD Students to Feel Valued

According to Maslow's (1968) Hierarchy of Needs, individuals must feel like they belong and are valued in order to reach their potential or self-actualize. However, GLD students often feel like a lower caste in the classroom because what is rewarded most in school are the very tasks that GLD students find difficult. If continuous modifications have to be made for them to achieve, or assignments watered down to be successful, how can they feel efficacious? To create an environment that is truly dedicated to developing potential in students, we must value and respect individual differences by rewarding students for what they do well. The philosophy in such an environment is one of interdependence where students work in cooperative groups to achieve goals. All students are encouraged to develop their talents and are offered options for mastering the curriculum. In this environment a well-produced video production about life in the Amazon is as useful as a written essay on the same topic. As a result, no child will feel like a second class citizen and indeed the GLD student can excel. Try some of the following tips as a start to creating a nurturing environment.

1. Create a buddy system where the GLD student and a classmate can consult each other about directions, assignments, and feedback about performance.

2. Offer options to all students for communicating knowledge. Book reports can take many forms.

3. Use cooperative groups to accomplish curriculum objectives. In forming groups, make sure that GLD students are matched with students whose skills complement theirs. For instance, pair a reader with a writer. Make sure the learning outcomes of the group are communicated in a way that allows the GLD student to be an expert.

4. Create a bulletin board where students can place situations-wanted ads and help-wanted ads. This presents an opportunity for all students to advertise their strengths and seek help in areas of weakness. One ad might read, "Do you need a great cover to put on your social studies report? See Suzy, the local artist." Or, "Help wanted. I need someone to review what is assigned for homework, each afternoon before dismissal. If you have great organizational skills, please apply for the position."

Students may be given a certain number of coupons to use as payment for a job well done. Coupons can be accumulated to use to buy more services or perhaps purchase other rewards the teacher has listed. For instance, ten coupons might be exchanged for one night with no homework. Students can earn additional coupons for services they render or exceptional behaviors they show.

Managing Behavior

There are certain behavioral characteristics associated with children who have learning disabilities. Chief among them are their seeming inability to pay attention, sit still, or stay on task.

Another problem is their lack of skills necessary to be an independent learner. GLD students may become over dependent on adults to help them organize long term assignments into manageable tasks. The suggestions offered here are purposefully designed to provide a flexible structure necessary to offset these negative behavior patterns and to encourage independence.

1. Encourage students to assume responsibility for their learning. This requires students to participate in decisions regarding what is learned, how it is to be learned, and what mode of communication is preferred. In addition, these students must have a clear understanding of what is expected and by what criteria success will be determined. Contracts are particularly useful in communicating and recording expectations.

2. Provide management plans to assist students to organize long-term assignments. Such a plan lists the individual tasks to be covered, provides target due dates and possible resources. Initially, these plans should be very detailed and target dates monitored carefully. It is a good idea to sit with students to get them started because frequently students simply do not know how to begin. (See boxed example.)

3. Provide clear information about what behavior is acceptable. Do not allow these students to blame their misbehavior on the fact that they are hyperactive or that they are on medication. Encourage them to control behavior. A gentle touch on a shoulder by a classmate served to remind one student to pay attention when the teacher was giving directions. Another student was told by a mentor that if he wanted to be a member of the film production company, he had to control his behavior. The mentor continued to explain what control meant: listen, do not interrupt, and be considerate of others. The student agreed to those conditions. He also negotiated with his mentor that when he felt out of control, he could leave the group for a few minutes to regain control.

Environmental cues can structure behavior for GLD students. For instance, private offices can be created for independent work. Designate a round table for informal and small group discussions. Review rules to be enforced while at the table. If the student does not feel that he or she can behave accordingly, allow the option to leave the group. In this way the student is responsible for the consequences of his behavior. Another area of the room might be designated for less structured activities where talking, movement, and laughter are acceptable.

4. To enhance motivation, pair activities so that the less desirable task precedes a preferred

---

Example

Before our young historian began her study of "A Day in the Life of Jerusha Webster," we created a visual overview of the project. In this way, the student could have an image of the whole to guide her as she completed the individual steps. The visual plan is provided on page 110.

Next she signed a contract that delineated her responsibilities and kind of help she could expect from her teacher. (See Contract, page 111.)

Debra needed a way to organize her study, so the teacher helped Debra to develop a management plan. This plan consisted of a step-by-step procedure with due dates, resources, and self-evaluation of progress. A piece of that plan (Log) is shown on page 111. Because the teacher did not want Debra's poor handwriting to discourage her or impede the progress of the study, the teacher jotted down the entries as Debra dictated them. In addition, the management plan needs to be easily read as it guides the student through the project. Trying to read back phrases written in Debra's hand would make reading far more difficult than it already was for her. Writing the plan should not be more of a chore for the student than the project itself. This is not the time to teach handwriting; it is most important that the student get beyond the weakness and into her research. Notice that little reading or writing was needed to complete the project. She used primary resources to get her information and presented it through drama.

task. The children become task oriented and efficient in accomplishing the first task in order to have time for the preferred activity. This strategy worked particularly well for a group of GLD students who elected to use rub-on letters to give their project a professional look. Using rub-on letters is tedious and far from exciting. However, the students eagerly attacked the task because they knew they would have time to enlarge some photographs in the darkroom as soon as they were finished. It should be noted that they did the lettering task in several small units rather than finish the complete task in one sitting.

Other students were given *extra* time to work on architectural models they were building with Legos™ upon successful completion of classroom assignments. Interesting results of this contingency were that not only did the quality of student work improve, but the time needed to complete assignments decreased.

5. Provide sufficient time for involved students to work without interruption. It is extremely frustrating to a student totally involved in learning or creating to have to stop because of artificial time constraints. Contrary to popular belief, GLD students have great concentration and can work for long periods of time in areas of strength and interest. The potential derived from intensive involvement in creative production might be worth a missed gym class or spelling lesson.

6. Be sensitive to students' frustration levels. Provide appropriate escape routes where GLD students can admit that a task may be too difficult while preserving integrity. For example, one student with poor motor coordination had a difficult time using rub-on letters. Totally frustrated with the task, he volunteered to go to the library to survey children's books for possible publishers and record their names and addresses. It took him an hour to complete the task. In essence, he negotiated a way in which he could contribute meaningfully to the group effort while avoiding failure.

Social and Emotional Concerns

Another vital component to include in the curriculum for GLD students is training them to understand and cope with the unique problems faced

The Plan Must Fit Together
Problem Focusing

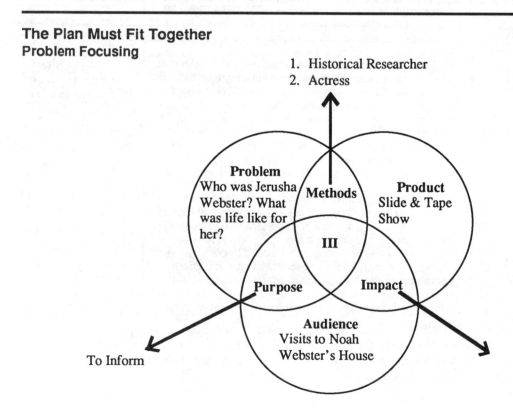

1. Historical Researcher
2. Actress

Problem
Who was Jerusha Webster? What was life like for her?

Methods

Product
Slide & Tape Show

III

Purpose

Impact

Audience
Visits to Noah Webster's House

To Inform

Contract

Beginning Date
March 3
Ending Date
May 18

Purpose of study:

   To add to knowledge of life in Colonial times.

Resources:

   1. Mr. Barron
   2. Collections—Noah Webster House
   3. Picture books—history books

Final Product:

   Slide & tape show "A Day in the Life of Jerusha Webster"

Target audience:

   Visitors at the Noah Webster House

Interim conference dates:

   Weekly on Wednesdays at 11:00

Teacher

Student

Log

Date	Task	Accomplished
3/14	Call for information Public Library 525-9121 Capitol 566-3662 Old State House 236-5621	✔
3/21	Call Webster House for appointment Prepare questions	✔
4/3	Visit Noah Webster House	✔
4/10	Interview Curator (Bring tape & questions)	✔
4/17	Look at books —History —Picture books —Filmstrip from school library	✔
4/25	Take slides of me in costumes at N.W. House	✔
5/2	Arrange slides Practice Sheet Check with curator	✔ ✔ ✔
5/9	Get tape and music for background	✔
5/10-5/17	Tape at home	✔
5/25	Show it to class	✔
6/1	Take to Noah Webster House	✔
	Party	

by GLD students because of the severe discrepancy between their strengths and weaknesses. Regularly scheduled "rap" sessions give GLD studnets an excellent opportunity to confront their problems and together develop strategies for facing them. The following describes a rap session program developed by Susan Katz, a classroom teacher who was concerned about the bright students in her class who were learning disabled.

Rap Sessions—A Model

Rap sessions are structured communication experiences with small groups who share a special need. These sessions provide a safe and non-threatening experience that fulfills the students' needs for involvement, relevance and thinking. Conducting rap sessions on a regular basis will help teachers to stay in touch with what is going on in these students internal world and help them to structure the environment they require for learning.

Rap sessions should satisfy certain goals. These goals include the following:

1. Developing the students' self-esteem by providing opportunities to be listened to and accepted by others;
2. Building trusting and caring relationships between teacher and student and among the students themselves;
3. Building communication skills: listening, verbal fluency, and language development (often areas of disability for GLD students);
4. Helping students identify areas of giftedness;
5. Alerting the GLD students to their potential worth in society;
6. Helping the students to discover ways to compensate for a problematic weakness;
7. Teaching the students to become their own advocates;
8. Fostering self-efficacy—the expectation that a particular task can be mastered (see Chapter 4).

Following are specific guidelines to follow when conducting a rap session:

1. Sit in a circle
2. Conduct an informal conversation in which students wait for the last person to finish speaking
3. Put downs, criticism or gossip are outlawed.
4. Confidentiality is assured
5. Everyone is entitled to give an opinion

The teacher's role in a rap session is to serve as the facilitator of interaction among the students. It is a time for teachers to listen and learn about the students—not a time to moralize or correct them. This is not an easy task for it requires sensitivity in areas where the student feels especially vulnerable. It also requires anticipating the possible avenues that the discussion might take. In addition, the teacher must be a good group discussion leader prepared to direct and redirect the rap.

The key to teachers' successes as facilitators of class discussions is their ability to formulate good questions. Here are some suggestions for possible discussion topics for GLD students in grades four and up.

• What is a learning disability? What is a smart kid? What does smart mean? If someone says you are smart, what do they mean? Can you be smart and have a learning problem? What are special problems do we have?

• What is hard about being learning disabled and smart? What is hard about being very good at some things but not others? If you were a teacher and had a gifted student with a learning problem, what are some of the things you would do? would not do? Suppose a kid had difficulty reading; how would you handle it?

• In what different kinds of ways do people communicate? How can people communicate without talking? without writing? Which ones are you best at doing? Which do you enjoy most when others do them? What are the advantages of communicating in different ways?

• Why do people not do their work? Do you ever make up excuses for not doing your work? Why is it hard for you to do a big project? How can you make sure you finish something you start? Is not being able to read a good excuse? Is thinking that you cannot do it a good excuse? Are excuses acceptable?

• Do adults have to do everything well? Who are some people you learned about who had a learning problem and succeeded in spite of it? How did they compensate for their disability? If you were a friend to that person, how could you help? How can we help one another in this group? In our class?

• What happens when teachers do not understand what it means to be smart and have a learning disability? How can you communicate your difficulty to your teachers? When should you try to talk to your teachers about your problems? What can you tell your teachers about how you learn and communicate best? Can you offer some suggestions to your teacher that would help you be more successful in school?

This book is our attempt to report what we have learned in the past ten years working with and studying the population of gifted, learning-disabled children. We hope that we have convinced you that these students are in need of appropriate attention. We believe that much more can be gained by emphasizing the strengths and interests of these students. Skills for success as creative, productive adults will be more easily acquired when learning is made relevant and put into context meaningful to the student.

We know that for these students to become successful adults, they will need to believe in themselves and their abilities. They must be made aware of their strengths and weaknesses so that they can set realistic goals. You will need to help them to understand the role of effort and to choose environments that will nurture and validate them.

We are fortunate today that institutions of higher learning are knowledgeable and sensitive to the needs of bright learning-disabled students. Scores on entrance exams are being replaced by analysis of individual IQ test such as the WISC-R of the Wechsler Adult Intelligence Scale (WAIS). Support programs are in place at many colleges and universities. For more information on this topic, we encourage the reader to take advantage of the many resources now available.

For instance, *Peterson's Guide to Colleges with Programs for Learning-Disabled Students*, using the same format of information that marks their other Guides, emphasizes institutions providing support for LD students. And another source, *A Guide to Colleges for Learning-Disabled Students,* edited by Mary Ann Liscio, surveys exactly what is available to LD students at the postsecondary level. The volume outlines costs, additional services offered, and modifications to traditional learning environment. It is most informative and should be of great assistance to counselors, parents, and the LD student. In addition we have included in Appendix E a bibliography of papers aimed at helping LD students find success in college. These papers, available for purchase, were produced by the Post-secondary Learning Disability Unit of the University of Connecticut's Special Education Center.

Epilogue

What happens when a student finally learns to become his own advocate and begins to make choices in his life that accentuate his gifts and talents? As we described in Chapter 1, Neil was a bright, creative youngster who was failing desperately in high school. His talent was photography. He especially enjoyed using his camera to study people: their joys, sorrows, and thoughts. With help from a tutor, Neil did graduate from high school. Both his tutor and his psychologist helped Neil to understand his disability and his strengths. They taught him compensation strategies and made him aware of the possibilities in his life. The psychologist was particularly helpful in pointing out colleges and universities that had programs in photography and support services for LD students.

However, Neil was not ready to accept the fact that he had a disability or, for that matter, that school was for him. He also made a decision that photography would remain his personal creative outlet, not to be compromised or exploited by the "outside world." His negative attitude toward school and his unwillingness to consider his options all were factors in supporting Neil's decision not to go to college immediately. The summer after graduation found Neil painting houses and reading. That summer he read three books: an autobiography of Richard Nixon, a biography of Abba Eban and one about the Holocaust. He remarked that now that school was over he finally had time to learn.

The next year found Neil unsuccessful at finding a job that he felt was worthwhile. He began to see the need for further education as a means of accomplishing his goals. He subsequently enrolled in a local college and began to take the traditional required courses. Although he was able to pass the courses on his own, he finally was convinced that he did have a disability. He explained, "I am not stupid. As a matter of fact, I am probably smarter than most of the kids here. Because I have a learning disability, things are more difficult for me. I have to put forth more effort and allocate more time for getting assignments done."

After two and a half years attending this school, Neil felt like he was getting nowhere. The curriculum left him flat. His peers and professors were uninspiring, and he felt like he was attending a "diploma factory." He stopped attending classes and completing assignments. Rather than ruin his record by failing, he decided to withdraw from school altogether.

Over the next year Neil worked for his dad while he did some serious thinking about what he wanted to do with his life. He examined what kind of learning environment would nurture his values, learning strengths, and intellect. He questioned people he respected, other students with similar interests, and other knowledgeable sources. He finally made up his mind to attend Sara Lawrence University. He was first admitted as a nonmatriculated student. He made up his mind that he would show his professors and himself as well, that he could excel. And excel he did! He was admitted on a conditional basis because the school was not convinced that his interest and productivity could be sustained. The next semester, however, he was formally admitted to the program. At this time he has one semester remaining to complete his degree.

To what does Neil attribute his new determination, task commitment and academic achievement? Neil believes that several factors have contributed to his success. First and foremost, is that he finally set a goal for himself that was meaningful to him. Second, he understood what kind of learning environment he needed. Specifically, Neil wanted an environment that respected his intellectual ability where courses would be challenging and relevant. He desired a learning environment where his peers were his intellectual equals and how, like himself, valued individual differences. Third, he wanted a school that cared about the individual and did not impose a universal structure on students. Last, he wanted a school that encouraged independent studies, projects and ongoing personal evaluation over exams and letter grades.

Sara Lawrence provides such an environment. Students attend small seminars where students loose their anonymity. As Neil phrases it, "You become very involved in your learning because there is no choice." In addition to seminars, independent studies are required in which students meet individually with the professor on a frequent basis. Students also interview prospective professors as part of their decision-making process in choosing courses.

When asked what his plans were upon completing school, Neil admitted that he was not certain. He felt that he would like to work for an organization whose major goals were to reduce prejudice and inequities in the world. He can see himself as someone who can make a difference. "No, I'm not concerned about my ability to do well in my life. Sara Lawrence really puts you in touch with what you can and cannot do. The professors build your confidence about your ability to succeed. I really feel that this unique experience has brought me to realize my fullest potential as a student. Most important, it has provided me with the courage to reach my potential as a productive adult."

Indeed, through Neil we can see the ideas conveyed in this book come alive. Neil's self-awareness, his commitment to become a self-actualized adult, and his courage to create an environment that validates who he is were crucial to his success. To Neil and others like him, we wish success and hope.

APPENDIX A

SEAT: Self-Efficacy for Academic Tasks

by S.V. Owen and S.M. Baum

Instructions for Administering the SEAT

The portions in *italics* should be read aloud to the students.

Step 1

(The purpose of this step is to determine how each child rates his/her ability to perform the behaviors listed.)

The paper lists some things kids do in school. I want you to tell me how good you are at these things. For example, if I ask about WRITING A REPORT, you decide whether you are good at writing a report, just okay at writing a report or bad at writing a report. Look at the faces on the paper. A smiling face means you are good at something , and a frowning face means you are bad at it. The face in the middle means that you are okay or average. For each behavior, circle the face that you think best describes how well you do that thing. I will read the first one aloud, and you circle the face that best describes how well you do at the activity.

Read the first item aloud, and wait for the children to circle the face chosen.

Are there any questions?

Read the rest of the behaviors, and ask them to choose one face that best describes how well they do that activity. Do all 34 items this way. Do not pay any attention to any of the other words under the faces for now.

Walk through the group and check to see if each child is proceeding correctly. Only after all the children have completed the first step, go on to Step 2.

(The purpose of the final two steps is to determine the child's perception, or attribution, for success at the things s/he does well.)

Step 2

Now look at your paper. You have circled different faces. Find the first happy face you circled. Please think about why you are good at that activity. Is it because you are smart, because you try very hard, because you are lucky, or because the activity is easy? After you decide, circle the most important reason that you are good at that task. Only choose one reason.

Now do the same for each activity where you circled with a happy face.

STOP AND WAIT FOR ALL CHILDREN TO COMPLETE THIS SECTION. Walk through the group and check to see if each child is proceeding correctly. Only after all the children have completed the first step go onto Step 3.

Step 3

Look at the paper one last time, but this time find the first frowning face you circled. Now decide why you are not good at this task. Is it you don't feel smart, because you do not try hard, because you are unlucky, because the task is too hard, or because you are shy? Decide which of these reasons is the best and circle the reason.

Do the same thing for the rest of the frowning faces you circled.

Grade_____**Boy [   ] or Girl [   ] Name**_____

WHAT GRADES DO YOU USUALLY GET IN SCHOOL? (Check one)

[ ] A's	[ ] A's and B's	[ ] B's
[ ] B's and C's	[ ] C's	[ ] C's and D's
[ ] D's	[ ] D's and F's	[ ] F's

HOW GOOD ARE YOU AT THESE THINGS?

1. Writing a report

Smart	Try Hard	Lucky	Easy		Not Smart	Don't Try	Unlucky	Too Hard	Too Shy

2. Teaching other kids

Smart	Try Hard	Lucky	Easy		Not Smart	Don't Try	Unlucky	Too Hard	Too Shy

3. Answering when a teacher calls on you

Smart	Try Hard	Lucky	Easy		Not Smart	Don't Try	Unlucky	Too Hard	Too Shy

4. Talking to other students about a school subject

Smart	Try Hard	Lucky	Easy		Not Smart	Don't Try	Unlucky	Too Hard	Too Shy

5. Talking to a teacher about a school subject

Smart	Try Hard	Lucky	Easy		Not Smart	Don't Try	Unlucky	Too Hard	Too Shy

6. Doing social studies projects

Smart	Try Hard	Lucky	Easy		Not Smart	Don't Try	Unlucky	Too Hard	Too Shy

7. Talking about a subject in front of the class

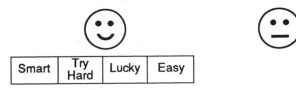

8. Doing homework

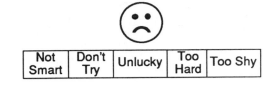

9. Taking important tests

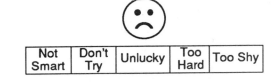

10. Obeying class rules

11. Taking short tests the teacher gives

12. Using a dictionary

13. Writing a letter

  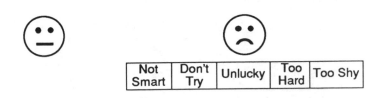

14. Doing art projects

Smart	Try Hard	Lucky	Easy

Not Smart	Don't Try	Unlucky	Too Hard	Too Shy

15. Taking part in music activities

Smart	Try Hard	Lucky	Easy

Not Smart	Don't Try	Unlucky	Too Hard	Too Shy

16. Doing a science experiment

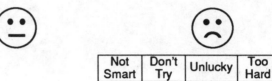

Smart	Try Hard	Lucky	Easy

Not Smart	Don't Try	Unlucky	Too Hard	Too Shy

17. Paying attention when a teacher is talking about a subject

Smart	Try Hard	Lucky	Easy

Not Smart	Don't Try	Unlucky	Too Hard	Too Shy

18. Following directions

Smart	Try Hard	Lucky	Easy

Not Smart	Don't Try	Unlucky	Too Hard	Too Shy

19. Asking questions in front of the class

Smart	Try Hard	Lucky	Easy

Not Smart	Don't Try	Unlucky	Too Hard	Too Shy

20. Writing a story or poem

Smart	Try Hard	Lucky	Easy

Not Smart	Don't Try	Unlucky	Too Hard	Too Shy

21. Solving math word problems

Smart	Try Hard	Lucky	Easy

Not Smart	Don't Try	Unlucky	Too Hard	Too Shy

22. Knowing math facts

Smart	Try Hard	Lucky	Easy

Not Smart	Don't Try	Unlucky	Too Hard	Too Shy

23. Writing neatly

Smart	Try Hard	Lucky	Easy

Not Smart	Don't Try	Unlucky	Too Hard	Too Shy

24. Reading aloud in front of other students

Smart	Try Hard	Lucky	Easy

Not Smart	Don't Try	Unlucky	Too Hard	Too Shy

25. Reading silently

Smart	Try Hard	Lucky	Easy

Not Smart	Don't Try	Unlucky	Too Hard	Too Shy

26. Reading library books

Smart	Try Hard	Lucky	Easy

Not Smart	Don't Try	Unlucky	Too Hard	Too Shy

27. Doing workbook pages in reading

Smart	Try Hard	Lucky	Easy

Not Smart	Don't Try	Unlucky	Too Hard	Too Shy

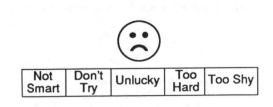
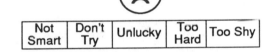
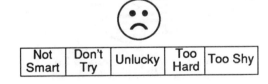

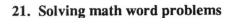

28. Playing games in gym

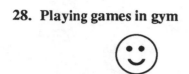 

Smart	Try Hard	Lucky	Easy

Not Smart	Don't Try	Unlucky	Too Hard	Too Shy

29. Working on a computer

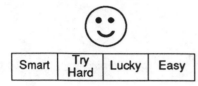 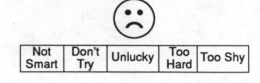

Smart	Try Hard	Lucky	Easy

Not Smart	Don't Try	Unlucky	Too Hard	Too Shy

30. Spelling

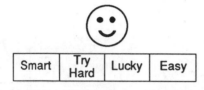 

Smart	Try Hard	Lucky	Easy

Not Smart	Don't Try	Unlucky	Too Hard	Too Shy

31. Finishing seatwork

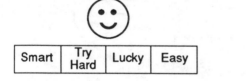 

Smart	Try Hard	Lucky	Easy

Not Smart	Don't Try	Unlucky	Too Hard	Too Shy

32. Doing exercises in gym class

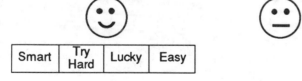 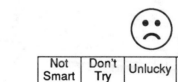

Smart	Try Hard	Lucky	Easy

Not Smart	Don't Try	Unlucky	Too Hard	Too Shy

33. Working with other kids in class

 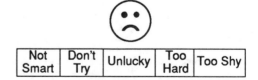

Smart	Try Hard	Lucky	Easy

Not Smart	Don't Try	Unlucky	Too Hard	Too Shy

34. Doing a report on a school subject

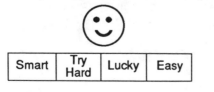 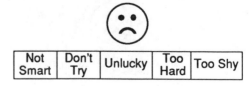

Smart	Try Hard	Lucky	Easy

Not Smart	Don't Try	Unlucky	Too Hard	Too Shy

Scoring the SEAT

Eleven scores can be derived from the SEAT. The first two describe the student's perception of competence on school-related tasks. The other nine are percentages reflecting how often a student offers a particular reason for an academic success or failure.

Directions for Scoring the Self-Efficacy Ratings

1. **Overall sense of academic self-efficacy**
   - Count the number of times the happy face was chosen and multiply that sum by three.
   - Count the number of times the neutral face was chosen and multiply that sum by two.
   - Total the number of frowning faces chosen.
   - Total the weighted scores from each category above to determine the overall score.

2. **Sense of academic failure**
   - Total the number of frowning faces chosen.

Table A.1   Average SEAT scores for various groups (grades 4–6)

	Gifted students	LD students	GLD students
Overall Self-efficacy	91	79	78
Academic Failure	1	4	6

Directions for Deriving Attribution Scores

1. **Success explanations**
   - Count the number of Success perceptions (Happy faces chosen).
   - Total the number of each attribute selected to explain success.
   - Divide each attribution total by the number of successes (from first step) to determine percentage of times a particular attribution is given. Because there are four possible explanations for success, there will be four percentages possible. Of course, if the child does not choose a particular explanation, the child will have a percentage explanation of zero.

2. **Failure explanations**
   - Count the number of frowning faces chosen.
   - Count the number of times each failure attribution was selected. Note that there are five choices for failure.
   - Divide each attribution for failure total by the number of total failures to determine the percentage that particular attribution was chosen to explain a failure experience.

Table A.2   **Average group attribution percentage scores**

	Gifted	LD	GLD
Success—ability	31%	29%	23%
Success—effort	31%	32%	41%
Success—ease of effort	37%	28%	37%
Success—luck	2%	7%	3%
Failure—lack of ability	5%	5%	2%
Failure—lack of effort	17%	29%	25%
Failure—task difficulty	15%	21%	33%
Failure—bad luck	5%	6%	11%
Failure—shyness	3%	14%	26%

APPENDIX B

Ways of Learning*

by John Dixon

"Ways of Learning" is an instrument created to allow school children to describe their way of thinking and learning in a structured way. It is not intended to be used as a way of generating norm-based scores for comparison with a wide assortment of other children or as a basis for determining which children should be served in a gifted education program. Rather, it is intended as a means for children, their parents, and their teachers to come to understand how it is possible to be both gifted and learning disabled at the same time. The distinctions in thinking style made in this instrument tend to be those which learning-disabled children experience as the way they are distinct from other children. By administering "Ways of Learning" and then reviewing the meaning of the selections the child has made, first with the child, then, perhaps, with the child's parents, a teacher has a powerful way of communicating to all concerned what it is that makes the child special and gifted, and to do this based on descriptions which the child has provided in language which everyone concerned can understand.

Each item in the "Ways of Learning" consists of two statements from which the child chooses the one which is most descriptive of the child. The items have been constructed based on considerable experience with gifted, learning-disabled children. In this experience it has been found that these children tend to pick the statements on the right side more often than other children. What this means in descriptive terms is that the children see themselves as spatially-mechanically inclined, creative, independent thinkers, appreciating global-integrative understandings, and enjoying a behavioral ease in the classroom—with different children emphasizing one or another of these characteristics. To put this in simple numerical terms, in one study, GLD children as a group chose 77% of the statements on the right side, a group of non-gifted LD children chose 63% on the right side, and a group of unselected school children in the same age range chose 60%. While this indicates that all school children have a tendency toward statements on the right, the difference in the GLD children represents a highly significant difference. It has been observed that many of the most gifted of the LD children we have worked with tended to pick nearly all of the statements on the right side.

While the instrument is set up with the statements of primary interest on the right side of each pair for ease of scoring and interpretation, administering it that way would allow the possibility of children getting into patterned responding and thus lead to faulty information. The best way to administer "Ways of Learning" with LD children is individually with each child, having the teacher read each item. While this is very time consuming for a teacher, it helps assure that children who have reading difficulties will be less likely to make language errors in interpreting the questions, and it also allows the teacher to get into discussions with a child which will help clarify and illustrate for the teacher what kind of experiences lead a child to respond in a given way. This kind of talk about the items during the administration has proved extremely enlightening. Teachers of the GLD often come away from this conversation with a very different perspective on what a child is really like; very different from the view the teacher had when the child was primarily seen as disabled.

---

* This instrument has not been fully validated and is for experimental use.

Many of the items are closely related to the distinction between Integrative Intelligence and Dispersive Intelligence discussed in Chapter 6. Keeping this distinction in mind during the administration, a teacher can get clearer insights as to why a child is disabled in some respects, but very gifted in others—and all from the experiential point of view of the child. The five separate dimensions used in "Ways of Learning" often correspond to scores on intelligence and creativity tests. For example, a child who indicates a strong preference for Visual-Spatial-Mechanical Thinking will often have appropriately high scores on the Block Design and Object Assemble scales of the WISC-R. Likewise, children who indicate a preference for Creative Production and Independent Thinking will often have correspondingly high scores on the Torrance Tests of Creativity. Children who indicate a preference for Global-Integrative Understanding may tend to have higher scores on the more abstract scales on the WISC-R such as Similarities or Comprehension.

If these kinds of correspondences between "Ways of Learning" and ability testing hold true, one might ask, why would a teacher want to use "Ways of Learning"? It is just an extra bother. In our experience it is not, precisely because it allows children, parents and teachers to communicate about the experiences of a child in terms that are commonly understandable rather than in terms of the obscure implications of test score numbers. Self-understanding is essential to the progress of the GLD child, and proper perspective is essential for a parent to be of assistance. For a teacher to be able to facilitate this through believable information derived directly from the child and place in new, understandable terms constitutes a powerful tool in the education of the gifted, learning-disabled child.

Administration

"Ways of Learning" might be explained to a child something like this:

> Some people do things best one way, and others do things best another way. I would like to know how you do things best. I am going to read you pairs of statements describing two different ways that a person might be good at doing things. After each pair, tell me which one best describes you. Both statements might actually describe you. In that case, choose the one which is most like you, and I will circle that statement. Let's try the first pair.

Remember to alternate which of the two statements is read first so that the child is less likely to get into responding patterns which are not truly based on the content of each item.

Scoring

Make sure that all items have been completed before scoring. At the end of each sections, count the number of statements which the child has selected from the right column. Then divide this by the total number of items in that section. If not all of the items have been completed, divide by the number which have. This will give you the proportion of items in the section which the child has chosen in the direction which is commonly found among GLD children. The pattern of proportions from each of the five sections provides a profile for seeing which of the common indications observed in these children is most consistently present. These profiles can help a teacher think about the kinds of activities which are likely to be of most benefit to a particular child. A listing of the profiles for all of the children in a program can help in thinking about groupings for specialized gifted activities and also in thinking about what children will have the greatest feeling of commonality.

Visual-Spatial-Mechanical Thinking

I enjoy writing about something interesting	1	I enjoy drawing something interesting
I remember something best through names and words	2	I remember something best through pictures in my mind
I learn to do something best if someone explains it to me	3	I learn to do something best if someone demonstrates how it is done
I help others learn best by talking to them about it	4	I help others learn best by showing them how to do it
Written explanations are best for me in learning something	5	Pictures and graphs are best for me in learning something
I get lost easily in places I have never been before	6	I find my way around easily in places I have never been before
I give directions best by describing them	7	I give directions best by drawing a map
I usually need directions or help putting a new toy together	8	I can often figure out how to put a new toy together just by looking at its parts
I would like memorizing lines for a part in a play	9	I would like decorating a stage or making costumes for a play
I would like being an actor in a movie	10	I would like running a camera for making a movie
I solve a problem best by talking it over	11	I solve a problem best by picturing the things involved in my mind
It is best for me to have the right tools for putting a mechanical thing together	12	I can often put a mechanical thing together even when I don't have the right tools

Count number of selections of right side
for Visual-Spatial-Mechanical Thinking_____
Divide by 12 =_____

Creative Production

When I learn a new idea, it is good to accept it the way it is	13	When I learn a new idea, I often push beyond it and create my own version
In math class I usually solve problems the way the teacher taught me	14	In math class I often make up my own way to solve a problem
I like learning about ideas which are known for sure	15	Even ideas which I am unsure about can be interesting
It is good for me to know the right way to solve a problem	16	Sometimes playing around at a problem can be a good way to solve it.
If I made up a story, poem or song, it would be because someone asked me to	17	Sometimes I make up stories, poems or songs just because I want to
I have a few new and different ideas	18	I have many new and different ideas
When I construct something I like to use materials made especially for that job	19	When I construct something, I can often use whatever materials I can find

Count number of selections of right side for Creative Production_____

Divide by 7 =_____

Global Integrative Thinking

When I learn something, I like getting into all the facts a student should know	20	When I learn something, I like to concentrate on the main ideas which make the subject important
It can be a waste of time thinking about the problems of the world	21	I sometimes think a lot about the problems of the world
I like to notice very closely the way people behave	22	I often try to figure out why people act the way they do
When something important happens in the world, I like to learn all I can about the details and facts of it	23	When something important happens in the world, I think a lot about what will happen because of it
I like to just enjoy movies and popular songs, not be concerned about their message	24	When I see a movie or listen to a popular song, I like to think about the message in it
In history class I like getting into all of the details of historical events	25	In history class I like to figure out why an event occurred

Count number of selections of right side for Global-Integrative_____

Divide by 6 =_____

Independent Thinking

I am best at thinking of ideas when I am with my friends	26	I am best at thinking of ideas when I am alone to concentrate
I like classes in which the teacher decides ahead of time the work that will be done	27	I like classes in which students make many decisions about the work they do
The things that others tell me can be important in making up my mind	28	I usually decide things based on my own thoughts and experiences
I like learning about things other people have created	29	I like trying to create something of my own
It is fun solving problems when I know ahead of time I can do it	30	It is fun trying to solve problems which are beyond what I am sure I can do
I don't like guessing at the answer to a problem because I could be wrong	31	I can often make correct guesses at the answer to a problem

Count number of selections of right side for Independent Thinking_____

Divide by 6 =_____

Behavioral Ease

It is fun to have discussions in class	32	It is fun to have active classes—to be doing things
I usually don't use gestures and movements when I talk	33	I often use gestures and movements when I talk
I like telling others about something I would like to make	34	I like just going ahead and constructing it
I enjoy talking with other people about my opinions	35	I would rather just go ahead and act on my opinions
I usually remember the things I am supposed to do	36	I sometimes forget the things I am supposed to do
I like working in a small, cozy place	37	I like working in a big, open room
I think best when I am sitting upright	38	I think best when lying down or walking
When I talk, the words almost always come out in the right order	39	When I talk, I sometimes have trouble getting words to come out in the right order
Students should be serious about their school work	40	Students should have a good time in school

Count number of selections of right side for Behavioral Ease_____

Divide by 9 =_____

Profile for the Five Scales

(Record the proportion of selections on the right side for each of the five scales as computed above)

Visual-Spatial-Mechanical Thinking_____

Creative Production_____

Independent Thinking_____

Global Integrative Thinking_____

Behavioral Ease_____

This profile provides a good indication of the strengths and interests of a GLD child which can guide a teacher in planning activities. In our work with many GLD children, we have found these kinds of insights derived form the child's own self-awareness to be very helpful in curriculum planning.

The following chart comments on the various activity considerations that should be made from the strengths that are revealed by "Ways of Learning."

High score in	Comments
Visual-Spatial-Mechanical Thinking	Provide activities such as Odyssey of the Mind, Science Fair, and Invention Convention.
Creative Production	Activities such as movie making
Independent Thinking	Individualized activities, **not** something like movie making which requires interpersonal cooperation
Global Integrative Thinking	Activities of philosophical or social issues
Behavioral Ease	Behavior of a child with the need for behavioral ease may appear to be impulsive, undisciplined and loose on occasions. While the child may need help keeping this within bounds, the behavior may also be highly involved in the child's creative capacities, and the teacher needs to think about how to guide the child toward achieving a balance.

APPENDIX C

Myself and Others*

by John Dixon

People get along with their friends in many different ways. Below are 37 questions which ask you about the ways you like to get along with your friends. For each question, choose between the two answers. Circle the one answer which is most like you. Please do not skip a question.

1. Do you usually like to study together with other students, or by yourself?

   With other students   *By myself*

2. When you decide something important, do you usually want to talk it over with others, or do you usually want to make the decision entirely on your own?

   Talk with others   *Make decision on my own*

3. Do you sometimes enjoy getting so involved in things that you don't care if you are not with your friends, or do you usually like to involve your friends in what you are doing?

   Usually want to involve friends   *Can forget friends when involved*

4. Do you sometimes feel bad that you are expected to do things for your friends?

   Very seldom   *Sometimes*

5. When you are invited to go someplace where there will be lots of people, do you usually look forward to going, or usually wish you had a reason for not going?

   Look forward to going   *Look for reason not to go*

6. Do you usually enjoy talking to other people, or does it often take an effort?

   Usually enjoy talking to others   *Often takes an effort*

7. Are there times when you most enjoy being by yourself, or is that seldom the case?

   Seldom the case   *At times I enjoy being myself*

8. Can you usually succeed in getting your friends to do what you want them to, or is that often difficult?

   Usually succeed   *Often it is difficult*

9. Do you sometimes enjoy doing things which will be considered odd to other people, or do you seldom care about such things?

   Seldom care   *Sometimes enjoy seeming odd*

* This instrument, cited in Chapter 6, is still in the developmental stage. Because LD students are known to have difficulty with social behaviors, it is included for your use. If you would like to participate in its development, please contact John Dixon.

10. Do you find that other students usually return your favors, or are you often disappointed?

    Favors are usually returned   *Often disappointed*

11. When you are having a conversation with another person, do you often have trouble thinking of things to talk about, or is that seldom true?

    Seldom   *Often*

12. Do you sometimes dislike feeling pressured by other people to act in a certain way, or is that seldom true?

    Very seldom   *Sometimes*

13. Can you usually convince your friends that your opinion is correct, or is that often difficult?

    Usually convince friends   *Often difficult*

14. Do you usually enjoy being the leader of groups you are in, or would you rather not be bothered?

    Enjoy being leader   *Rather not be bothered*

15. Do you think it is usually correct to try to have the same opinions as the friends you are with, or should a person think more on their own at all times?

    Have same opinions as those you are with Always think more on your own

16. Does it take you a while to feel comfortable with people you have never met before, or does that come fairly quickly?

    Comes quickly   *Takes a while*

17. When you have a difference of opinion with a friend, is it often true that you succeed in changing the friends mind, or is that usually not what happens?

    Often change friends mind   *Usually not*

18. When you are with a group, do you like being the center of attention?

    Yes   *No*

19. Is getting up in front of a class to give a speech usually difficult for you or usually easy?

    Easy   *Difficult*

20. When you meet a new person, is it a struggle figuring out what to say to that person, or is it easy?

    Easy   *A struggle*

21. When you are participating in an important ceremony in which people are all dressed up and acting in special ways, do you have difficulty figuring out what to do with yourself?

    No   *Yes*

22. Do you feel good when people notice how you are dressed and comment on it, or a little embarrassed?

    Good   *A little embarrassed*

23. Do you usually like people who fit in and do things the way others do it, or are you more likely to enjoy people who like to be different?

    Like those who fit in   *Enjoy those who are different*

24. Do you find that your wishes are often different from other peoples, or are they usually the same?

    Usually the same   *Often different*

25. Is it easy for you to praise something that another person has done, or do you often hold back?

    Easy to praise   *Often different*

26. Do you often stop to think to yourself why another person has said something, or do you usually consider thinking about it a waste of time?

    It is a waste of time   *Often think about other peoples reasons*

27. When you are watching other people, do you often try to figure out why they do what they do, or is that a bother?

    That's a bother   *Often try to figure out why*

28. Are you more interested in what people do, or why they do it?

    What they do   *Why they do it*

29. When is it easier for you to find the right words for something, when you are talking or writing?

    Talking   *Writing*

30. When you are with a group of friends, would you rather talk or listen?

    Talk   *Listen*

31. When you have an opinion, can you usually change it easily, or do you stick to it?

    Change easily   *Stick to it*

32. How much do you bother about the way you dress for school?

    A lot   *Not much*

33. If a person tends to be different from your friends, do you tend to avoid that person or be interested in that person?

    Avoid   *Be interested*

34. If you had a serious disagreement with a friend, would you still want to keep that friend or forget about the friendship?

Still be friends   *Forget about it*

35. Do you feel comfortable when your opinions agree with others you are with, or doesn't it matter?

Feel comfortable with same opinions   *It doesn't matter*

36. Do other people consider you talkative or quiet?

Talkative   *Quiet*

37. When you make a new friend, is it usually you who has made the most effort?

Yes   *No*

APPENDIX D

Structured Interview

1. Describe this child's interests.

2. Have you observed situations in which this child	
• becomes totally absorbed in a particular subject area?	Yes / No If yes, please explain
• has discussed adult topics such as politics, religion, or current events?	Yes / No If yes, please explain
• becomes self-assertive, stubborn or aggressive?	Yes / No If yes, please explain
• avoided tasks?	Yes / No If yes, please explain
• was particularly curious?	Yes / No If yes, please explain
• was highly imaginative?	Yes / No If yes, please explain
• was humorous or seemed to be aware of nuances of humor?	Yes / No If yes, please explain

APPENDIX E

Special Education Center Publications

The Postsecondary Learning Disability Unit of the University of Connecticut's Special Education Center has produced a number of papers, reports, and materials regarding adolescents and adults with learning disabilities. The following documents are now available (on a pre-paid basis) for the cost of reproduction, postage, and handling.

For more information contact
Special Education Center Publications
The University of Connecticut, U–64
249 Glenbrook Road
Storrs, CT 06269-2064

Orders must be pre-paid. Make checks payable to Special Education Center

Document Number	Title, Author, and Description
LDC 2	The University of Connecticut Program for Learning Disabled College Students: Final Report." (1986). Norlander, K.A., Czajkowski, A., & Shaw, S. Reproduced by ERIC Document Reproduction Service No. 278 194, 1987.
	This is a report of a two-year effort to develop a model program of services for learning-disabled students in a university setting. Program goals and procedures are described and appendices include forms and program documents.
LDC 4	*McGuire-Shaw Postsecondary Selection Guide and Manual for Learning Disabled Students.* (1986). McGuire, J., & Shaw, S. A Manual B Specimen Set (Manual; 1–Part I; 6–Parts II & III; 2–Part IV) C Sample Set (1 each–Parts I, II, III, IV) D Set of 10 (Parts I-IV) E Sets of 10, any single Part (I or II or III or IV)
	The McGuire-Shaw Guide is a tool to assist college-bound learning-disabled students in selecting a suitable college or university. By considering a student's strengths and weaknesses as well as anticipated support services in a post-secondary setting, a process which takes into consideration characteristics of the institution as well as the LD support program can result in informed decision making for future educational and career goals. This Guide is designed for use by students, parents, LD high school personnel, guidance counselors, and independent consultants.
LDC 5	"A Decision-Making Process for the College-Bound Student: Matching Learner, Institution, and Support Program." (1986). McGuire, J., & Shaw, S. Published in Learning *Disability Quarterly,* 1987, *10,* 106–111.
	This article describes a process designed to help college-bound students with learning disabilities select an appropriate postsecondary setting.
LDC 7	"Designing Support Services and Instruction for College Students with Learning Disabilities: Use of Diagnostic Data." (1988). Anderson, P., Norlander, K., Shaw, S., Nottingham, J., Segal, L., & Spillane, S. Published in D. Knapke & C. Lendman (Eds.), *Capitalizing on the future,* (pp. 59–64). Columbus, OH: AHSSPPE.
	This paper addresses this need to design individualized support services for college students with learning disabilities based upon sound diagnostic/prescriptive evaluation data. In addition, program issues including remedial versus compensatory instructional services and helping students work toward independence are discussed.

Document Number	Title, Author, and Description
LDC 8	"Training Leadership Personnel for Learning Disability College Programs: Preservice and Inservice Models." (1986). Shaw, S., Norlander, K., & McGuire, J. Published in *Teacher Education and Special Education*, 1987, *10*, 108–112. This manuscript discusses the competencies needed by postsecondary learning disability leadership personnel and describes current preservice and inservice training efforts.
LDC 9	"Diagnosis and Program Selection for College Students with Learning Disabilities." (1987). Norlander, K.., Shaw, S., McGuire, J., & Czajkowski, A. This manuscript describes a psychoeducational evaluation process which effectively delineates the academic and learning strengths and weaknesses of college students with learning disabilities. These evaluation data are used in a systematic approach to match the characteristics of the student to the postsecondary institution and learning disabilities support program.
LDC 10	"A Bibliography of Postsecondary Programming for Students with Learning Disabilities." (1988). Shaw, S.F., & Shaw, S.R. A current bibliography of more than two hundred references on LD college student characteristics, diagnosis, programming, transition, interventions, and evaluation.
LDC 11	"Accommodations for College Students with Learning Disabilities: The Law and Its Implementation." (1985). Brinckerhoff, L. Published in J. Gartner (Ed.), *Tomorrow is another day*, (pp. 89–95). Columbus, OH: AHSSPPE. This paper overviews Section 504 and litigation which has shaped the concept of "reasonable accommodations" for postsecondary students with learning disabilities. Specific examples of suitable academic adjustments are described.
LDC 12	"Evaluating College Programs for Learning Disabled Students: An Approach for Adaptation." (1988). McGuire, J.M., Harris, M., & Bieber, N. Published in D. Knapke & C. Lendman (Eds.), *Capitalizing on the future*, (pp. 53–58). Columbus, OH: AHSSPPEE. This article presents a comprehensive approach use in Connecticut to develop an evaluation design suitable for programs in two- and four-year settings. Based upon adaptation of Stufflebeam's *et al.*, (1972) CIPP model, process and product evaluation activities were conducted to investigate program effectiveness and identify areas for consideration in meeting student needs.
LDC 13	"Postsecondary Education for Students with Learning Disabilities: Forecasting Challenges for the Future." (1989). McGuire, J., Norlander, K., & Shaw, S. This article identifies challenges to the field of learning disabilities which will seriously affect access to higher education for students with learning disabilities. The paper levels with a call for policy formulation, research, and administrative planning for change.
LDC 14	"Competencies of Postsecondary Education Personnel Serving Students with Learning Disabilities." (1989). Norlander, K., Shaw, S., & McGuire, J. This paper presents the results of a national survey designed to identify the needed competencies of both administrative and direct service personnel in directing and implementing postsecondary support programs for students with learning disabilities.
LDC 16	"Preparation of Students with Learning Disabilities for Postsecondary Education." (1988). Shaw, S., Norlander, K., McGuire, J., Byron, J. & Anderson, P. Paper presented at the 66th Annual CEC Convention, Washington, DC. This paper suggests alternatives for enhancing secondary programs for the learning disabled. Modifications in the secondary school program are proposed including the early development of postsecondary transition plans, the focus of resource rooms on learning strategies and social skills training instead of content tutoring, and effective counseling to develop a match between the unique needs of the student and an appropriate postsecondary training opportunity.

Document Number	Title, Author, and Description
LDC 17	"Critical Issues in Learning Disability College Programming." (1988). Brinckerhoff, L., Shaw, S., Norlander, K., & McGuire, J. Published in D. Knapke & C. Lendman (Eds.), Celebrate *in '88...AHSSPPE and all that jazz,* (pp. 19–40). Columbus, OH: AHSSPPEE This article describes approaches for garnering administrative support and funding, interpreting and using diagnostic data and measuring the success of support programs for students with learning disabilities.
LDC 18	"Preparing Students with Learning Disabilities for Postsecondary Education: Issues and Future Needs." (1989). Shaw, S., Brinckerhoff, L., Kistler, J., & McGuire, J. The transition from high school to postsecondary education for students with learning disabilities requires a sense of independence founded on strong self-advocacy skills and an ability to transfer learning strategies across curricular boundaries and into the real world. This article presents issues that parents and secondary educators must address to nurture the independence necessary for the transition to postsecondary education and adult life.
LDC 19	"Interpreting LD Diagnostic Reports for Appropriate Service Delivery." (1989). Anderson, P., & Brinckerhoff, L. Paper presented at the 12th National Conference of AHSSPPE, Seattle, WA This article demonstrate how learning disability service providers can use a student profile chart to identify pertinent data from psychoeducational and neurological reports and use it to match individual student needs with appropriate support services.
LDC 20	"Implementing Regional Consortia for Postsecondary Learning Disability Personnel." (1989). Brinckerhoff, L. Shaw, S., & McGuire, J. Paper presented at the 12th National Conference of AHSSPPE, Seattle, WA. This paper describes an effective technique for expanding the networking opportunities of LD service providers in postsecondary education. By developing state or regional consortia, LD service providers can share resources and information, and establish informal channels of communication.
LDC 21	"Resource Guide of Support Services for Students with Learning Disabilities in Connecticut Colleges and Universities." (1989). McGuire, J., & Shaw, S. (Eds.). This resource guide developed through a grant from the Connecticut Department of Higher Education, provides complete and up-to-date information on services for students with learning disabilities at 41 colleges and universities within the state of Connecticut.
LDC 22	"Providing Learning disabilities Service at Technical Colleges: A New Challenge." (1989). McGuire, J., & Bieber, N.. Paper presented at the 12th National Conference of AHSSPPE, Seattle, WA. This paper provides an overview of the needs identified in five Connecticut technical colleges through twelve months of on-site technical assistance. A comparison of the typical two-year community college and the technical college on selected variables offers insight into some important differences that should be considered by service providers.
LDC 23	"A Field-Based Study of the Direct Service Needs of College Students with Learning Disabilities." (1989). McGuire, J., Hall, D., & Litt, V. This descriptive study conducted with students with learning disabilities in a large university setting provides an overview of their specific support service needs with implications for student services personnel. The results of this study may also be useful to secondary school personnel in better preparing college-bound students with learning disabilities.

Special Education Center Publications
Order Form

Shipping Information—PLEASE PRINT

Name: _____

Address: _____

City: _____ State: _____ Zip: _____

No.	Title	Quantity	Unit Price	Total Price
LDC 2	"The University of Connecticut Program for Learning Disabled College Students: Final Report"	_____	$10.00	_____
LDC 4	*McGuire-Shaw Postsecondary Selection Guide and Manual for Learning Disabled Students*			
	LDC 4A Manual	_____	$10.00	_____
	LDC 4B Specimen Set (Manual; 1–Part I; 6–Parts II & III; 2–Part IV)	_____	$14.00	_____
	LDC 4C Sample Set (1 each–Parts I, II, III, IV)	_____	$4.00	_____
	LDC 4D Set of 10 (Parts I-IV)	_____	$20.00	_____
	LDC 4E Sets of 10, any single Part (I or II or III or IV)	_____	$6.00	_____
LDC 5	"A Decision-Making Process for the College-Bound Student: Matching Learner, Institution, and Support Program"	_____	$4.00	_____
LDC 7	"Designing Support Services and Instruction for College Students with Learning Disabilities: Use of Diagnostic Data"	_____	$4.00	_____
LDC 8	"Training Leadership Personnel for Learning Disability College Programs: Preservice and Inservice Models"	_____	$4.00	_____
LDC 9	"Diagnosis and Program Selection for College Students with Learning Disabilities"	_____	$4.00	_____
LDC 10	"A Bibliography of Postsecondary Programming for Students with Learning Disabilities"	_____	$4.00	_____
LDC 11	"Accommodations for College Students with Learning Disabilities: The Law and Its Implementation"	_____	$4.00	_____
LDC 12	"Evaluating College Programs for Learning Disabled Students: An Approach for Adaptation"	_____	$4.00	_____
LDC 13	"Postsecondary Education for Students with Learning Disabilities: Forecasting Challenges for the Future"	_____	$4.00	_____

Special Education Center Publications
Order Form (page 2)

No.	Title	Quantity	Unit Price	Total Price
LDC 14	"Competencies of Postsecondary Education Personnel Serving Students with Learning Disabilities"	_____	$4.00	_____
LDC 16	"Preparation of Students with Learning Disabilities for Postsecondary Education"	_____	$6.00	_____
LDC 17	"Critical Issues in Learning Disability College Programming"	_____	$4.00	_____
LDC 18	"Preparing Students with Learning Disabilities for Post-secondary Education: Issues and Future Needs"	_____	$4.00	_____
LDC 19	"Interpreting LD Diagnostic Reports for Appropriate Service Delivery"	_____	$4.00	_____
LDC 20	"Implementing Regional Consortia for Postsecondary Learning Disability Personnel"	_____	$4.00	_____
LDC 21	"Resource Guide of Support Services for Students with Learning Disabilities in Connecticut Colleges and Universities"	_____	$2.00	_____
LDC 22	"Providing Learning Disabilities Service at Technical Colleges: A New Challenge"	_____	$4.00	_____
LDC 23	"A Field-Based Study of the Direct Service Needs of College Students with Learning Disabilities"	_____	$4.00	_____

TOTAL ENCLOSED _____

▼ ORDERS MUST BE PREPAID ▼

Make checks payable to **Special Education Center**

Please forward your payment and order form to

**Special Education Center Publications
The University of Connecticut, U–64
249 Glenbrook Road
Storrs, CT 06269-2064**

Bibliography

American Psychiatric Association (1987). *Diagnostic and statistical manual of mental disorders* (3rd Ed., revised). Washington, DC.

Anderson, J.R. (1990). *Cognitive psychology and its implications* (3rd Ed.). New York: W.H. Freeman.

Asher, J. (1987). "Born to be shy?" *Psychology Today*, April, 56–64.

Ashton, P.T. & Webb, R.B. (1986). *Making a difference: Teachers' sense of efficacy and student achievement.* New York: Longman.

Association for Children and Adults with Learning Disabilities (1985). ACLD-proposed definition and rationale. LD Forum. Winter.

Baldwin, J.D. & Baldwin, J.I. (1987). *Behavior principles in everyday life* (2nd Ed.). Englewood Cliffs, NJ: Prentice-Hall.

Bandura, A. (1977). "Self-efficacy: Toward a unifying theory of behavior change." *Psychological Review, 84*, 191–215.

——————. (1986). *Social foundations of thought and action.* Englewood Cliffs, NJ: Prentice-Hall.

——————. (1989). "Human agency in social cognitive theory." *American Psychologist, 44*, 1175–1184.

Bannatyne, A. (1974). Diagnosis: A note on recategorization of the WISC-R Scaled scores. *Journal of Learning Disabilities, 7*, 272–274.

Baum, S. (1984). *Meeting the needs of gifted learning disabled students.* Roeper Review, 7, 16–19.

——————. (1985). *Learning disabled students with superior cognitive abilities: A validation study of descriptive behaviors.* Unpublished doctoral dissertation, University of Connecticut, Storrs.

——————. (1988). "An enrichment program for gifted learning disabled students." *Gifted Child Quarterly, 32*, 226–230.

Baum, S. & Dixon, J. (1985). Program for handicapped students who are gifted or talented. Funded project, Cheshire, CT: Connecticut State Department of Education.

Baum, S. & Owen, S. (1988). "High ability learning disable students: How are they different?" *Gifted Child Quarterly, 32*, 321–326

Black, H.E., & Black, S. (1984). *Building thinking skills*. Pacific Grove, CA: Midwest Publications.

Borkowski, J.G., Johnston, M.B., & Reid, M.K. (1987). "Metacognition, motivation, and controlled performance." In S.J. Ceci (Ed.), *Handbook of cognitive, social, and neuropsychological aspects of learning disabilities*, Volume II. Hillsdale, NJ: Erlbaum.

Borland, B. & Heckman, H. (1976). "Hyperactive boys and their brothers: A 25-year follow-up study." *Archives of General Psychiatry, 33*, 669-675.

Brigance, A.H. (1977). *Inventory of basic skills*. North Billerica, MA: Curriculum Associates, Inc.

Brophy, J.E. (1981). "Teacher praise: A functional analysis." *Review of Educational Research, 51*, 5–32.

Burks, S. Jansen, B. & Terman L. (1930). *The promise of youth: Follow-up studies of one thousand gifted children, genetic studies of genius*. Stanford, CA: Stanford University Press.

Chalfant, J. & Schefflin, M. (1969). *Central processing dysfunction in children: A review of research*. (NINDS Monograph No. 9). Bethesda, MD: U.S. Department of Health, Education and Welfare.

Chance, P. (1987). "Master of mastery." *Psychology Today, 21*, (4), 42–46.

Clarizo, H.F. & McCoy, G.F. (1984). *Behavior disorders in children* (3rd Ed.). New York: Harper & Row.

Clements, S. (1966). *Minimal brain dysfunction in children* (NINDB Monograph No. 3, Public Health Service, Bulletin No. 1415). Washington DC: U.S. Department of Health Education and Welfare.

Colarusso, R. & Hammill, D. (1972). *Motor-free visual perception test*. New York: Harcourt, Brace, Jovanovich.

Connolly, A. (1988). *Key math*. Circle Pines, MN: American Guidance Service, Inc.

Covington, M.V. & Omelich, C.L. (1977). "Effort: The double-edged sword in school achievement." *Journal of Educational Psychology, 71*, 169–182.

Cruickshank, W. (1966). *The teacher of brain-injured children: A discussion of the bases for competency*. Syracuse: Syracuse University Press.

Dixon, J. (1983). *The spatial child.* Springfield, IL: Charles C. Thomas

—————. (1986). *Myself and others.* New Haven, CT: Yale University, unpublished manuscript.

—————. (1986). *Ways of learning.* New Haven, CT: Yale University, unpublished manuscript.

—————. (1989). "Integrative intelligence: What is it and how is it measured? " Paper presented at 2nd Annual Conference for the Education of Gifted Underachieving Students. New Haven, CT: Yale University, May 5, 1989.

Dixon, J. & Baum, S. (1986). *Focus on talent: An enrichment program for gifted/LD students.* State funded grant, Project Rescue, Litchfield CT: Connecticut Department of Education.

Douglass, L.C. (1981). "Metamemory in learning disabled children: A clue to memory deficiencies." A paper presented at the annual meeting of the Society for Research in Child Development, Boston, MA.

Durrell, D.D. & Catterson, J.H. (1980). *Durrell analysis of reading difficulty.* New York: Harcourt, Brace, Jovanovich, Inc.

Farley, F. (1986). "The big T in personality." *Psychology Today,* March, 43ff.

Federal Register (1977). U.S. Office of Education. "Education of handicapped children." Federal Register, *42,* 65082–85.

Fox, L. (1983). "Gifted students with reading problems: An empirical study," in Fox, L., Brody, L., & Tobin, D. (eds.). *Learning-disabled/gifted children: Identification and programming.* Baltimore: University Park Press.

Gardner, H. (1983). *Frames of mind: The theory of multiple intelligences.* New York: Basic Books, Inc.

Gelzheiser, L.M. (1984). "Generalization from categorical memory tasks to prose by learning-disabled adolescents." *Journal of Educational Psychology, 76,* 1128–1138.

Getzels, J. & Jackson, P. (1962). *Creativity and intelligence: Explorations with gifted students.* New York: John Wiley.

Goldman, R., Fristoe, M., & Woodcock, R. (1970). *Goldman-Fristoe-Woodcock test of auditory discrimination.* Circle Pines, MN: American Guidance Service, Inc.

Good, T.L. , & Brophy, J.E. (1987). *Looking in classrooms* (4th Ed.). New York: Harper & Row.

Gordon, W. (1961). *Synectics: The development of creative capacity*. New York: Harper & Row.

——————. (1971). *The metaphorical way of learning and knowing*. Cambridge, MA: Porpoise Books.

Guilford, J.P. (1962). *Intelligence, creativity, and their educational implications*. San Diege, CA: Knapp

——————. (1959). "Three faces of intellect. " *American Psychologist, 14*, 469–479.

——————. (1967). *The nature of human intelligence*. New York: McGraw Hill.

Hammill, D.D. (1985). *Detroit tests of learning aptitude 2*. Austin, TX: Pro-Ed.

Hammill, D. Leigh, J., McNutt, S., & Larson, S. (1981). "A new definition of learning disabilities." *Learning Disability Quarterly, 4*, 336–342.

Harbar, J. (1981). "Learning disability research: How far have we progressed?" *Learning Disabilities Quarterly, 4*, 372–381.

Heimlich, J.E. & Pittleman, S.D. (1986). *Semantic mapping: Classroom applications*. Newark, DE: International Reading Association.

Herman, G. (1986). "Kinesthetic learners." Paper presented at summer Conference: Creating Gifted Behavior, Bowling Green State University, June 15.

Hildreth, G. (1966). *Introduction to the gifted*. New York: McGraw-Hill.

Hofstadter, D. (1985). *Metamagical themas*. New York: Basic Books.

Jastak, S. & Wilkinson, G. (1984). *The wide range achievemnet test-revised*. Wilmington, DE: Jastak Associates.

Kavale, K. & Nye, C. (1981). "Identification criteria for learning disabilities : A survey of the research literature." *Learning Disabilities Quarterly, 4*, 383–389.

Kirk, S. (1963). "Behavioral diagnosis and remediation of learning disabilities." In Conference on Exploration into the Problems of Perceptually Handicapped Children (pp. 1–7). Evanston, IL: Fund for Perceptually Handicapped Children.

Lewis, R., & Doorlag, D. (1983). *Teaching special students in the mainstream.* Columbus, OH: Charles E. Merrill.

Large, C. (1987). *The clustering approach to better essay writing.* Monroe, NY: Trillium Press.

Lawrence, S. & Hart, B. (1972). *Free to be you & me.* New York: Artista Records.

Licht, B.G. (1984). "Cognitive-motivational factors that contribute to the achievement of learning-disabled children." In J.K. Torgesen & G.M. Senf (eds.) *Annual review of learning disabilities (Vol 2).* New York: Professional Press, pp. 119–126.

Loftus, E.F. (1979). *Eyewitness testimony.* Cambridge, MA: Harvard University Press.

Loftus, E.F. & Palmer, J.C. (1974). "Reconstruction of automobile destruction: An example of the interaction between language and memory." *Journal of Verbal Learning and Verbal Behavior, 13* 585–589.

Luria, A. (1968). *The mind of a mnemonist.* New York: Basic Books.

MacKinnon, D. (1965). "Personality and realization of creative potential." *American Psychologist, 27,* 717 727.

Maker, C.J. 1977). *Providing programs for gifted handicapped.* Reston, VA: Council for Exceptional Children.

Marland, S. (1971) *Education of the gifted and talented.* Washington, DC: U.S. Office of Education, Department of Health, Education & Welfare.

Markwardt, F. (1989). *Peabody individual achievement test-revised.* Circle Pines, MN: American Guidance Service, Inc.

Maslow, A. (1968). *Toward a psychology of being* (2nd edition). Princeton, NJ: D. Van Nostrand.

McKim, R.H. (1980). "Experiences in visual thinking." (2nd edition). Monterey, CA: Brooks/Cole Publishing Company.

McLeod, J.A. (1965). "A comparison of WISC subtest scores of preadolescent successful and unsuccessful readers." *Australian Journal of Psychology. 17,* 220–228.

Miller, G.A. (1956). "The magical number seven, plus or minus two: Some limits on our capacity for processing information." *Psychological Review, 63,* 81–96.

Olson, J & Mealor, D. (1981). "Learning disabilities identification: Do researchers have the answer?" *Learning Disability Quarterly, 4*, 389–392.

Owen, S.V. & Froman, R.D. (1988). "Development of a college academic self-efficacy scale." A paper presented at the annual meeting of the National Council on Measurement in Education, New Orleans.

P.L. 94–142, (1975). Education for All Handicapped Children Act, S. 6, 94th Congress [See 613 (a) (4)] 1st session, June. Report No. 94–168.

P.L. 95–561, Title IX, Part A. (1978). The gifted and talented children's education act of 1978, Section 902.

Parnes, S. Noller, R. & Biondi (1976). *Creative Action Book.* New York: Charles Scribner's Sons.

Poplin, M. (1981). "The severely learning disabled: Neglected or forgotten?" *Learning Disability Quarterly, 4*, 330–335.

Renzulli, J.S. (1977). *The Enrichment Triad Model: A guide for developing defensible programs for gifted and talented.* Mansfield Center, CT: Creative Learning Press, Inc.

——————. (1978) "What makes giftedness: Re-examining a definition." *Phi Delta Kappan, 60*, 180–184, 261.

——————. (1985). "The three-ring conception of giftedness: A developmental model for creative productivity," in Sternberg, R., & Davidson, J. (Eds.). *Conceptions of giftedness*, New York: Cambridge University Press.

Renzulli, J.S., Reis, S.M., & Smith, L.H. (1981). *The revolving door identification model.* Mansfield Center, CT: Creative Learning Press, Inc.

Renzulli, J.S., & Reis, S.M. (1985). *The schoolwide enrichment model: A comprehensive plan for educational excellence.* Mansfield Center, CT: Creative Learning Press, Inc.

Renzulli, J.S., Smith, L.H., White, A.J., Callahan, C.M. & Hartman, R.K. (1977). *Scales for Rating the Behavioral Characteristics of Superior Students.* Mansfield Center, CT: Creative Learning Press, Inc.

Rico, G.L. (1983). *Writing the natural way.* Los Angeles: J.P. Archer.

Roe, A. (1953). *The making of a scientist.* New York: Dodd Mead.

Ross, D.,& Ross, S. (1982). *Hyperactivity: Current issues, research and theory*. New York: Wiley.

Schiff, M., Kaufman, N., & Kaufman, A. (1981). "Scatter analysis of WISC-R profiles for LD children with superior intelligence." *Journal of Learning Disabilities*.

Schunk, D.H. (1983). "Ability versus effort attributional feedback: Differential effects on self-efficacy and achievement." *Journal of Educational Psychology, 75*, 348–856

Schunk, D.H., & Cox, P.D. (1986). "Strategy training and attributional feedback with learning disabled students." *Journal of Educational Psychology, 78*, 201–209.

Schunk, D.H., & Lilly, M.W. (1984). "Sex difference in self-efficacy and attributions: Influence of performance feedback." *Journal of Early Adolescence, 4*, 203–213.

Shepard, L. Smith, M., Vojir, C. (1983). "Characteristics of pupils identified as learning disabled." *American Educational Research Journal, 20*, 309–331.

Silverman, L. (1989). "Invisible gifts, invisible handicaps." *Roeper Review, 12*, 37–41.

Slavin, R.E. (1986). *Educational Psychology*. Englewood Cliffs, NJ: Prentice Hall.

Slosson, R. & Nicholson, C. (1990). *Slosson oral reading test*. East Aurora, NY: Slosson Educational Publications.

Stevens, G., & Birch, J. (1957). "A proposal for clarification of the terminology used to describe brain-injured children." *Exceptional Children, 23*, 346–349.

Strauss, A.E., & Lehtinen, L. (1947). *Psychopathology and Education of the brain-injured child*. New York: Grune & Stratton.

Tannenbaum, A. (1983). *Gifted children: Psychological and educational perspectives*. New York: Macmillan.

Taylor, C. (1986). "Cultivating simultaneous student growth in both multiple creative talents and knowledge." in Renzulli (ed.) *Systems and models for developing programs for gifted and talented*. Mansfield Center, CT: Creative Learning Press, Inc.

Terman, L. (1926). *Genetic study of genius: Mental and physical traits of a thousand gifted children*. Stanford, CA: Stanford University Press.

—————. (1959). *Genetic studies of genius: The gifted group at mid-life*. Stanford, CA: Stanford University Press.

Terman, L. , & Oden, M. (1947). *Genetic studies of genius: The gifted child grows up: Twenty-five years' follow-up of a superior group, Vol. 4.* Stanford, CA: Stanford University Press.

Torrance, E.P. (1972). *Torrance Tests of creative thinking.* Bensenville, IL: Scholastic Testing, Inc.

Treat, L. (1983). *You're the detective.* Boston: David R. Godine.

Triesman, A.M. (1964). "Monitoring and storage of irrelevant messages in selective attention." *Journal of Verbal Learning and Verbal Behavior, 3,* 449–459.

Wallach, M.A. (1976). "Tests tell us little about talent." *American Scientist. 64,* 57–63.

Wechsler, D.A. (1974). *Wechsler Intelligence Scale for Children-Revised.* New York: The Psychological Corporation.

Weiner, B. (1972). "Attribution theory, achievement motivation, and the educational process." *Review of Educational Research, 42,* 203–215.

—————. (1979). "A theory of motivation for some classroom experiences." *Journal of Educational Psychology, 71,* 3-25.

Weiner, B., Graham, S., Taylor, S.E., & Meyer, W. (1983). "Social cognition in the classroom." *Educational Psychologist, 18,* 109–124.

Wepman, A. (1975). *Auditory discrimination test.* Chicago: Language Research Association, Inc.

Whitmore, J. (1980). *Giftedness Conflict and Underachievement.* Boston: Allyn & Bacon.

Witty, P.A. (1958). "Who are the gifted?" In N.B. Henry (ed.), *Fifty-seventh yearbook of the National Honor Society of Education, Part II.* Chicago: The University of Chicago Press.

Ysseldyke, J.E. (1983). "Current practices in making psychoeducational decisions about learning disabled students." *Journal of Learning Disabilities, 16,* 226–233.

Zimmerman, B. (1989). "A social cognitive view of self-regulated academic learning." *Journal of Educational Psychology. 81,* 329–339.

Zukow, A.H. (1975). "Helping the hyperkinetic child." *Today's Education, 63,* 39–41.

Index